Stella Milner

STRANGERS

STRANGERS

A FAMILY ROMANCE

BY EMMA TENNANT

A NEW DIRECTIONS BOOK

Publisher's Note: New Directions owes special thanks to Alexandra Pringle for first suggesting *Strangers*.

Photographs for Chapters 4 (page 63) and 9 (page 151) are copyright Cecil Beaton, reproduced by courtesy of Sotheby's London. Photograph for Chapter 5 (page 83) is copyright Derek Hill, reproduced by permission of Derek Hill.

Manufactured in the United States of America
New Directions Books are printed on acid-free paper.
First published in the U.K. in 1998 by Jonathan Cape. First published
by New Directions clothbound in 1999.

Library of Congress Cataloging-in-Publication Data

Strangers : a family romance / Emma Tennant.
     p. cm.
ISBN 0-8112-1409-5 (alk. paper)
1. Tennant, Emma—Family.   2. Women novelists, Scottish—20th century—
Family relationships.   3. Family—Scotland—Borders Region—History—
20th century.   4. Asquith, Margot, 1864-1945—Family.   5. Tennant family.
I. Title.
PR6070.E52Z477   1999
823.914—dc21   98-51105
                              CIP

SECOND PRINTING

New Directions Books are published for James Laughlin
by New Directions Publishing Corporation
80 Eighth Avenue, New York 10011

. . . In psychoanalysis [this] is known as the pubertal child's 'family romance'. These are fantasies or daydreams which the normal youngster partly recognises as such, but nonetheless also partly believes. They centre on the idea that one's parents are not really one's parents . . . and one has been reduced to living with these people, who *claim* to be one's parents. These daydreams take various forms: often only one parent is thought to be a false one . . .

Bruno Bettelheim,
The Uses of Enchantment

CONTENTS

PART ONE

PAMELA'S JEWELS

For daughters have morning when mothers have night,
And there's Beauty alive when the fairest is dead.
As when one sparkling wave do sink down from the light,
Another do rise up to catch'n instead.

William Barnes, from The *White Wallet*,
an anthology of prose and poetry
edited by Pamela Glenconner, 1912

ONE

Pamela

Pamela Tennant in 1907 with her children: (*l. to r.*)
Clare, Christopher, Stephen and Bim.

Here they are, in the inevitable photograph. Uncle Jack lies back on the tartan rug with a lordly air, as if the squares of brown, mauve and dim green wool beneath him were emblems of the division of money, land and estates he will one day inherit – for all that he is only the third son. Uncle Frank has had a glass of port too many, to chase down the rough delicacies of a shooting picnic: his eye is trained on the steep road that leads away from the shepherd's cottage and the nibbled grass where they are sitting. The thought of the afternoon drive bores him; he wants to go home. Cousin John, the busy one who has come from Glasgow to shoot grouse in the presence of a Prime Minister, cranes forward, as far as possible from the younger sons and, like a row of trees, the legs of the keepers standing behind them in hairy stockings. Cousin John is making his own pile, in the works that no-one now mentions. His cross, pudgy face shows his annoyance at being excluded from the front row of this momentous photograph.

It's August 1912, the twelfth of August, known as the 'Glorious Twelfth'; and the front row of this group is glorious indeed. Eddy – Lord Glenconner – is taller and more handsome than his brothers: his hair is crinkly like theirs, but, unlike theirs, it is blond and the curls look intentional. His wife Pamela, the famous beauty, sits dreamily at his side. She is, as always, in white: today the simple white lawn dress has a cape of cream-coloured wool over it, to keep her from the piercing cold of a Scottish summer. Her expression is one of self-immolation, of consciousness of the wifely duty she is performing by being there at all. For on the far side of Eddy sits his sister, Margot, and relations are strained between the sisters-in-law. Margot has a beak nose and a fiery wit. She makes it plain whenever she can that she pities her brother for being married to Pamela, who gives him so little of her love and has an unhealthy obsession with her children. If it weren't for the fact that Margot is married to the Prime Minister, who came on the night train from London with his red boxes and Uncle Jack, his Private Secretary, to attend the Glorious Twelfth on his brother-in-law's moor, Pamela would have found an excuse to stay at home. Stephen, her youngest, can be counted on to come up with a fever or a bad cough that needs the attentions of his mother, on these occasions. But today, even though Stephen displayed all the required symptoms at the sight of men in plus-fours and of wagons with dogs and guns, Pamela has left him and gone to join the photograph. Her head is slightly inclined in the direction of the Prime Minister, who sits on the far side of Margot, his other neighbour a tall pile of dead birds.

Bim is with the children, right in the front of the picture; and it's clear the photographer has had difficulty with them, because the land slopes away at this point from the party on the rug, and the children all appear to have large feet – something Pamela's daughter Clarissa – Clare – will be angry about right up to the day she dies. The children, although told by their father to keep absolutely still, are slightly out of focus, as if they were growing so fast the camera was unable to capture them: Bim, the eldest of the boys, his mother's pride and joy and at fifteen too grown up to sit with the children; Christopher (Kit), serious and dark, already sent away to sea and home on leave; Clare, the image of her mother and precociously wilful and sulky, just sixteen; and young David, who bears no resemblance to anyone. Pamela's jewels, her treasures: as the photographer presses down the shutter they turn, just a fraction, towards her; and perhaps it is this movement that throws a shadow across their young faces, blurs jawline and hair – a shadow that seems to show an ambivalence to the mother, who holds them close to her even as she smiles across her husband and Margot at her eminent guest.

The sun comes out just as the big box camera and tripod are being packed away. The sitters rise, stiff, from the bumpy ground, and a swarm of small bees chases Uncle Frank into the shepherd's cottage, where he pours himself a brandy from the decanter. The head keeper comes forward, with an allotment of butts for the men to stand in and search the skies for game. Margot's strident laugh rings out and is caught in the valley, where nothing meets the eye but straggling woods and an expanse of heather, home of the birds that will be sacrificed on this all-important day.

A young woman comes out of the back room of the shepherd's croft to pick up and fold the rug and pack away the picnic things still left on the grass. A smell of sheep's pellets fills the air as she shakes the rug free; and then the smell of wood burning, as Kit and

David light a bonfire and throw on sticks and bracken. Pamela calls to them to be careful. Then, in a different, gracious voice, she thanks the photographer for his services – and in another voice again asks the Prime Minister if she can accompany him to the place in the heather where he will stand half-concealed as the birds come over. The young woman, who is a maid at the Big House, asks Her Ladyship if she wishes to take the rug with her, on the moor.

Pamela's voice this time is light and teasing. 'Bim will carry it for me – won't you, my darling?'

For all the clarity of her gaze, in the photograph that is now as brown and faded as the walls of the unused bathroom where it hangs – at the top of the house, where no-one ever goes – Pamela is blind to the look that passes between the maid and her eldest son. She accepts his sweet acceptance of his role as carrier of the rug with no more than the faintest of smiles; a smile that seems to freeze the young woman, who kneels, packing a wicker basket with china plates, each stamped with its gold laurel wreath and family crest.

'Tell Stephen I'll be back in time for tea, won't you, Louisa?' are the parting words of Pamela to the young woman, as she goes off arm-in-arm with her son, to join Mr Asquith on the moor.

The house lies in a pool of stillness, of expectancy. Soon it will be evening, and time for dinner: shadows lengthen on the grass outside and will linger, blue, until late; roses and lilies give off scent from the garden, and heather from the hills, with a whiff of honeysuckle from the brae that runs up to Maggie Cunningham's post office. The yellow tiles of the courtyard, freshly washed down, gleam ready for the tyres of Eddy's new Lanchester. The trees in the many-tiered garden, mostly beech and silver birch, wave leaves that are as crisp and clean as newly printed money. Everything is perfect here – even if Pamela doesn't think so, but prefers the South, where the downs are more calming to her soul.

Louisa goes round the house, preparing it for evening. She has to do this and wait at table as well, for Maudie Renshaw and Janet Vaughan are both down with influenza in the village, and Her Ladyship won't have menservants, it's a well-known foible of hers. Until the women are better, Louisa must do their work, and hers as well. She breathes noisily as she goes up one staircase and down another, and comes out on the main landing, where Mrs Asquith has her room, and the Prime Minister his dressing-room opposite. Louisa goes in and draws the heavy yellow silk curtains, and turns on the lamps so that the room, like a stage set, is suddenly ready for night, for jingling an evening bag with a beaded fringe and sweeping out in a dress with a narrow waist and a full, striped skirt. Is it time to draw the bath? Janet does this, generally, and Louisa pauses, unsure, in the vast bathroom Sir Charles Tennant, His Lordship's father, installed, along with twenty others, in this house that was built as a monument to his fortune and success. Louisa goes and closes the mahogany and wicker lid to the lavatory, a throne with arms, set on a pedestal. Behind her, the sky in the bathroom window comes in still light as innocent day – surely the water would be cold if she were to fill the bath now and add the salts that sit packed in a glass jar on the rosewood table? She decides to wait; and turns to see herself in the glass, which descends from the ceiling to meet a wide wash-basin, resplendent with lemon verbena soaps and hung with freshly ironed Irish linen hand-towels.

Louisa practises a smile – a smile such as Pamela might wear, calm, unworldly, compassionate – but sees instead a grin spread across a freckled face, on which a blush suddenly appears, as footsteps are heard outside in the passage. Heavens, it's later than she thought! The pale blue of the sky in the window has turned, treacherously, to an evening darkness; the house throbs with rising and falling feet, as family and guests go to their rooms to change for dinner. There's a smell of gardenias, brought in from the greenhouses by McNeil, the gardener, for the gentlemen's buttonholes; and from the back stairs, when the door into the passage is opened by Mrs Wilson, the housekeeper, in search of the mooning Louisa, a mingling of gravy smells and singeing feathers, as today's game is plucked, trussed and drawn.

To escape Mrs Wilson, Louisa goes into the bedroom as the housekeeper knocks and then opens the bathroom door – and from the bedroom she slips into the passage and off towards the nursery, where no-one will think of looking for her. For a reason she knows well, but refuses to admit to herself, she is restless and rebellious tonight: she has already turned down the thick, crisp sheets on Pamela's bed and laid out the tortoiseshell hair-brushes on the china tray on the dressing-table, where Pamela, in white voile, sits and looks into the perfection of her face. Louisa has been up and down the back stairs, where the bachelors' quarters lead off gloomy landings; she has seen to the needs of Mr Frank and Mr Jack, the diminutive brothers of His Lordship and uncles of her Bim. She has drawn the curtains in Mrs Asquith's room – very well then, the Prime Minister's wife will have to fill her own bath. Now, before she must don frilly apron and cap and wait at table as well, she will go to see Nanny Trusler as she tucks Stephen into bed.

The nursery, a three-windowed room that looks out on the garden at the point where it rises to the road that goes along the hills, still holds on to daytime: the curtains, stiff with William Morris's birds and berries and willow branches, are still drawn back; and in this light, which might have been invented just to lure children outdoors again, Kit and David, dawdling over their supper at the big, square table, look longingly out at fields where imagined rabbits run, to be chased and shot. Now their sister, Clare, the sole daughter in the family, comes in from her cold blue bedroom with the narrow four-poster next to the nursery, and goes to the window-sill to lean out into the darkening garden. She dreams of lights and carriages and cars there, of young men waiting to take her to the dance – when all that is there is a long breath of wind from the immense hills, their flagrant purple dimmed to brown by the dying light. She turns and snaps something at Louisa. Certainly it seems unfair, not to be allowed to come down to dinner, if you're spoilt and beautiful, like Clare. Bim will join the Prime Minister and the other guests at dinner: why not she? But Pamela, sensing the coming rebellion, has announced that her daughter's head cold has worsened after spending all day on the moors.

Nanny Trusler makes use of Louisa as soon as she sees her – Fill the water jug, dear – Pass Stephen's nightshirt, it's on the fender – Take Kit and David's plates to the sink – Wash them up while you're at it, Louisa, will you? And, as Louisa goes to the door in the corner of the nursery, which opens into a turret-shaped room converted with sink and draining-board to a place where the children's meals are washed up, after being cooked and carried all the way from the kitchen, she hears the tone of Nanny Trusler's voice change. Bim, the loved, the favourite, has come into the room. With clumsy hands reddened by scrubbing and polishing and cleaning and scouring, Louisa drops the plates into the sink with a dreadful clatter. David, the naughtiest, the least obedient of Pamela's children, laughs at the sound. But the restlessness in Louisa is, for the time being, assuaged, quietened. Bim has come in; and, picking up young Stephen, he tosses the angelic-looking child high in the air.

Nanny Trusler cries out in mock alarm. But she is contented, too: Bim brings with him a sense of evening, of anticipation. He switches on the lights, which glow on the walls in crystal tulips of glass and illuminate the plaster Madonna above the fireplace, in her blue robe. Nanny Trusler calls for Stephen to be set down – and the child, with his long, golden ringlets already acting the part of the daughter Pamela really wanted when he was born, cries out in feigned terror.

But Bim makes everyone gather round him. He soon has Kit and David and even Clare listening and whispering; and, when Nanny Trusler goes into the night-nursery, a 'conspiracy' is forged, to meet after dinner up on the roof, where only Bim is allowed to go unattended. What fun it will be! Louisa dries the plates – two are chipped from the fall, but none broken – and comes out of the turret cleaning-room with a surge of sudden, new confidence. Although it can't be so, she feels that Bim has come here this evening especially to find her. She looks him straight in the eye; and he looks gravely back at her, at fifteen as tall as he will ever be, with a faint pencilling of a moustache and a face so handsome that John Singer Sargent has already drawn it again and again. Bim takes after Pamela and not his father. Bim is Pamela's son: it's as if she's barred anyone else from being involved in the process of creating someone so perfect.

Bim smiles at Louisa. A gong sounds in the hall, the sound muffled by the heavy baize door that cuts off the nurseries from the rest of the house.

'Dinner!' Bim says, and Clare asks him for the hundredth time to plead with their mother to allow her to come down.

'But, sweetheart, you've eaten up here already,' says Nanny Trusler. And she sends Louisa down to the kitchen to see if there's any summer pudding left from yesterday for the children.

Louisa, as she flees down the back stairs, stops for just one moment and looks up – at the skylight, high above her, set in the roof, where, somewhere in all its dizzying levels, she will find Bim later, under the moon.

There are so many people seated in the dining-room that Louisa follows Bina, the head parlour-maid, with panicky steps. She has never waited at table, here, and it's quite different from Wilsford, the house in Wiltshire where Pamela's dream of simplicity permits just one maid handing at table, and very few courses of plain food. Here, the gold tree-candelabra, with the stags standing at the base as if caught in a forest of money, the rich carvings on ceiling and cornice, the cornucopias of fruit and flowers that crown the dining-room, and the high fireplace in green and red marble seem like a warning to those who would like to enter the family but have no right in it. Even the table, opened out with another leaf tonight to accommodate the Prime Minister and his wife, presents a code that is indecipherable to Louisa. Thin silver forks go from the fruit fork, frail at the outer edge of the place settings, to the medium fork for savouries and the like, and the sturdy fork for meat and game. Louisa has been told a hundred times how to arrange cutlery, and how to make a perfect globe from the linen napkins, crested like the knives and forks with a sailing-ship, a device conjured up by Eddy's father – but she never can remember how it goes. Her thoughts wander and she sets the side plate to the right of the mat, with its starched, frilly cover. Or she lines up the turreted pepper pots and mustard boats, with their blue glass linings, like an array of miniature soldiers in front of each guest. She's only half there, when it comes to serving this family whose fortune, crest and motto have been acquired so very recently. It's as if her own fortunes, as daughter of the kennel-man down the Back Road, have got muddled up with them somehow; and she finds herself upsetting the order of the dining-room like a wicked fairy, to remind them of the thin line between their antecedents and hers.

The line isn't thin at all, of course. For it's not only the money which pours in from Eddy's father's investments and mines and chemical works that distinguishes this family from her own; it's breeding, too. Pamela, who boasts French royal blood in her veins, was never in love with Eddy, some say, but at least he was rich, and she, in love with another, married him for that. Others say the match was made in Heaven: Eddy good-looking and good-humoured, and so much in love with the beautiful Pamela that he gives her anything she asks for. (And, for all her cultivation of simplicity, Pamela asks for a great deal.) Proof, anyway, of their success as a couple are the children, all so fascinating – if a little spoilt – and, most of all, Bim.

Louisa finds Bim at the far side of the table and watches him through a haze of candlelight. Bim the poet, the valiant, pure Bim, who is so clearly cut out

for an extraordinary life. He will serve his country –
no doubt about that – and Louisa sees Pamela watch
him too, as he replies to questions about his hopes for
the future, from Mr Asquith the Prime Minister. Even
Aunt Margot (Louisa thinks of Bim's relatives in this
way – to call them Aunt and Uncle and Papa in her
thoughts is to draw closer to him) looks on with
approval as Bim talks of poetry. Asked to quote from
The Iliad, he does so with modesty and finesse.

Uncle Frank, downing the white Pouilly Fuissé that
is poured to accompany the stuffed crab, leans
forward to catch Bim's quiet responses to further
questioning about his hopes for a career. How about
the Army? he says, his voice still tinged with the
Glasgow accent of his youth; and Louisa, removing
plates, feels her hand brush against Pamela's head, as
her agitated reaction comes. Of course Pamela will
not see her son going out to massacre people.
Inevitably Bim is destined to be a Leader in the
Movement towards Peace.

Uncle Frank mumbles and wipes his moustache
with his napkin. He looks imploringly at Louisa to
refill his glass. And, despite Margot's disapproving
glare, she does so. Uncle Jack sits as square and self-
important as a despatch box at the far end of the
table: his eyes dart constantly to the PM and he barks
his comments on any subject, whether invited to do
so or not. Eddy, joining in the conversation about
Bim's future, leans down the table towards his son
and his wife. They all smile together: how handsome,
how perfect they are! Louisa fills Uncle Frank's glass
in defiance of family disapproval. She knows Uncle
Frank feels as permanently excluded from this

powerful circle as she does. Anyway, it's quite fun when he has to be helped across the hall, as she has seen happen after dinner, and guided into the billiard room rather than embarrass his relations at their port.

Tonight, however, there are to be other diversions. The grouse comes in on a silver platter (the game should be hung for several days, but this is the Twelfth, after all, and the Prime Minister is here and has vanquished several birds); and there are murmurs of approval at the *garniture* of feathers tied to the rump of each bird, the sculpted silver sauce-boats (these carried awkwardly by Louisa), which follow the progression of the game round the table. The dishes contain bread sauce, crumbs and gravy. Louisa knows which she should offer first – but, as always, she forgets to offer the gravy at all. She sees Aunt Margot, who is in the midst of a scornful diatribe against women's suffrage, stare pointedly at her through the blaze of candlelight. And she knows she stands for what Margot hates most about the regime here, since the old Bart died and Eddy allowed his whim-struck wife to run the place. Women serving at table! Women – who are anathema to Margot (as she places with dry, brittle fingers a cigarette in the long amber holder, to smoke just as soon as the grouse has gone round) – women, who keep her poor husband awake at night, with their bombs and their smashed windows and their ludicrous fasts. Louisa's clumsy hands could belong only to a girl trained to feed shooting-dogs their oats; but here Margot stops her line of thought and digs the spoon deep into the bread sauce, which Louisa holds far too close to her, as if the wretch wanted to spill it all down her chest, encased in glittering jet beads. Margot decides to speak to Eddy about this monstrous affectation of maid-servants on the part of Pamela. There will be a disaster before dinner is over, that's plain to see.

The door opens and Nanny Trusler looks in. There's something undeniably comic about seeing Nanny in this setting, and Uncle Frank, well gone on the Château Palmer, gives a snort of laughter. What on earth can she be doing here? Is there a crisis, or has Clare set fire to the place with her curling tongs? Uncle Frank voices his opinions on the matter; then, as Nanny Trusler comes right into the room, with a timid look in the direction of Pamela at the foot of the table, he falls silent with the rest. It's as if Nanny Trusler, whose starched apron and blue blouse stand for an earlier order of things – a punishment meted out when deserved; a liquorice stick as a reward for good behaviour – has come to put the assembled company to bed. They have stayed up too late, they are indulging themselves in their own ways – ways Nanny Trusler knows only too well: Frank with his drinking; Jack bolting down his food, as if they hadn't been told often enough that only servants eat in silence; Eddy, Sir Edward now, of course, as round-shouldered as she always told him he would be. Even the Prime Minister, who had been in the midst of describing his yacht, *The Enchantress*, and its beauties to his brother-in-law, looks apprehensive at the sight of this figure of authority suddenly and unexpectedly amongst them. She is not demanding the vote – no, certainly not – but she is formidable for all that, she brings disruption with her, just as a calm, opulent evening away from the cares of office stretched ahead.

Margot is the only one with the courage to ask this visitor what is wrong. For Pamela, cheeks pale and eyes burning very dark at the end of the table, lives in a climate of fears and premonitions. You can see her glance at Bim, now, to make sure he's safely there, not the subject of Nanny Trusler's alarm. Her misty 'signals' – she's said to have seen ghosts in her mother's house down in the South, and to foresee disaster (for she has Irish blood too, of course: aren't Margot and the rest of the family tired of hearing about it?) – may have failed her tonight, or so her expression says, for she had seen nothing bad coming to them all. God, let it not be a fire, not another fire! The house burned to the ground six years ago and was built up again exactly as it was, for the old Bart would certainly not permit his life to be seen to end in a ruin. The thought causes Pamela to twist in her chair, away from Nanny Trusler, as if staring at the pointed, caustic faces of the portraits Eddy's father hung here – faces that were no forebears of his, but whose lace and delicate accoutrements gave him the air of a gentle past – could make the problem, what-ever it might be, go away. There was a crudeness, still, about life with Eddy's family: these powdered ladies and their red-faced husbands, unrefined though they undoubtedly were, would have sent Nanny Trusler from the room, dealt with the matter both more efficiently and with less sense of self-importance.

For Margot, exercising her right as elder sister of

Eddy, has risen to her feet and walked round the table to put an arm – a scraggy, authoritative arm – on Nanny Trusler's shoulder. (She is ruining the evening, Pamela always knew she would.) But there's no stopping Margot now. She bends down and invites the old nurse to confide in her. Really, it's too mawkish, like something in a Barrie play – or so thinks Uncle Frank, who chortles again at all the fuss. It's probably nothing more than Stephen with a temperature, calling for his mother, who spoils him and dresses him as a girl; Stephen, who insisted on sending for his mama. And here they all are, arrested just as the grouse, with those bright, splayed feet, are levered on to their plates.

Nanny Trusler speaks in a low voice to Margot – whose rudeness and precocity when a child are forgotten now she's so sophisticated, and married to the Leader of the country as well. She says Miss Clare has gone missing. Nanny Trusler found she wasn't in her room, and when she went down to the kitchen, McNeil the gardener came in and said he'd seen what he took to be Miss Clare walking fast down the Back Road, keeping away from the moonlight under the big trees.

She was with a man, Nanny Trusler says McNeil the gardener had said.

TWO

Margot

Margot Asquith, 1912

It is the summer of 1914. Margot lies dreaming, in the dark bedroom at 10 Downing Street she has disliked for six long years now. The dream takes different forms, but the theme is always the same: Violet, her stepdaughter, daughter of Mr Asquith and only too well aware of the fact, has come to take away Margot's possessions – even, on occasion, all her favourite rugs and pictures from the bright house in Cavendish Square, which had to be given up when Mr Asquith was appointed Prime Minister. Once, a few weeks back, the dream had taken the horrible guise of a fashion show, with Margot's dresses parading one by one in the dimly lit basement of the Premier's residence; the biscuit satins and black silks, the feathers and bunched taffetas then borne, as if on an invisible wire, out into the wastes of Whitehall and beyond.

That Violet is responsible – so her stepmother knows, but cannot bring herself to acknowledge – for the theft of her most valuable possession of all, the Prime Minister's heart, has been made dangerously clear in this latest instalment of the dream. Violet's best friend, a big tomboyish girl, Venetia Stanley by name, grinned at the Prime Minister's wife quite brazenly, just before Margot woke to her maid coming in. The soft rustle of coals followed by a crackle of fire brought their brief reassurance (Margot suffers from the cold: she is thin and bony as a stickleback and the morning ritual at the grate, reminiscent of her happy and protracted youth at Glen, can be counted on to banish the dream). But the effects of the new revelations and reminders of the night will return, as they always do, to ruin the day.

Violet and her friend Venetia have become as threatening in real life as they are in their victim's sleep. Margot knows it was no dream yesterday, when she walked down to the Prime Minister's room, to find him sitting in his leather chair with his usual calm, laughing and teasing the tall, awkward girls with puns and riddles, as if there weren't a choice of conflagrations on the cards. Civil war in Ireland – yes, Margot knows everyone is waiting for that. But something far worse – the European war – that may come too. Sir Edward Grey, the Foreign Secretary, is as non-committal as the Prime Minister on the subject. Yet Margot knows – as the insistent, provoking dream was anxious to underline – that her husband possesses far more intelligence of the intentions of the foreign powers than he is prepared to divulge to her. Of course he does! The trouble is, he no longer confides anything in his wife. Venetia, who has tucked a letter into her dress before giving that unpleasant smile this morning and then vanishing with the arrival of the maid and the first snap and lick of fire, into the realm Margot most despises and denies, the intangible kingdom of Mr Asquith's obsession and infatuation with his daughter's friend, is the recipient of the most weighty of the Prime Minister's confidences. He writes to her three times a day: from the House of Commons; from weekends at 'The Wharf'; from his bedroom, whence he has long been banished by Margot, who has difficulties with the bearing and birthing of children. He sends everything – military secrets, declarations of an undying love, childish games and puzzles – to this clever, ungainly girl. Margot may not be capable of guessing the extent of her husband's correspondence with Miss Stanley – but what she doesn't know is more than made up for by the dreams.

It has not been a good summer for Mrs Asquith. The women are insufferable, in their demand for the right to vote: Margot is sick of explaining at dinner parties that men and women should realise they are not of the same kind, but belong to different species. Mr Asquith's embracing of Home Rule for Ireland has led to social embarrassments previously unthinkable, in the settled, confined world of the 'Souls', to which coterie she has always belonged. How could Lord Curzon, for example, a Soul and one of her oldest friends, dare to exclude Mr and Mrs Asquith and their daughter Elizabeth from his ball in May? How depressing it is that fashionable London dines one against the other, all because of Ireland! Why can't people learn that the Prime Minister's view is invariably the right one (Margot is nothing if not loyal, to this member of another species), and if they are in doubt they can come to her and be told what to do. As wife of Head of Government, Margot has been known to summon Trades Union leaders to the Ritz Hotel and to write emotional letters to those who do not understand the policies of Mr Asquith.

Now the embarrassments appear to grow daily. Margot goes to the House – and a crowd gathers round her, avid for news of the coming war. Will it happen, or will it not? Surely Mrs Asquith will know.

It's a fact that Margot has sent her own daughter to Holland to stay with the late King's mistress, Mrs Keppel. If Elizabeth is free to travel around Europe in August, then there must be secret information available to the Prime Minister and his family, or they would never let the only daughter of Mr Asquith's famous second marriage go right through France at a moment like this. Clearly, there will not be a war. But at the same time, people are beginning to look oddly at Margot – can it be that she simply doesn't know? 'We are within measurable, or imaginable, distance of a real Armageddon,' Mr Asquith writes from the Front Bench to Venetia. And Margot, hurrying home through the crowds, takes to her bedroom again, to the solace of a summer fire and to a great pile of letters of her own. She is the wife of the Prime Minister, after all.

A summer brownness has settled over London. Elizabeth is still in Holland with Alice Keppel, whose pleasant air, along with the dove grey and pinks of her gowns, seems to preclude any possibility of war. It is time to go north. Surely Henry (as Margot has always called her husband; 'Herbert' has gone, even if his daughter Violet likes to address her communications to him in this way) – surely Henry must need his shooting this year, his Glorious Twelfth on the moors? Margot can feel the freshness of the wind over Gumscleuch, high in the hills bought by the old Bart and carefully seamed with Scots firs by his son

Eddy in preparation for the annual meeting. She hears the peewit – and then the grouse as it calls its 'Goback, Goback!' to the guns as they advance, some steady, others scrambling on heather and scree. Why has Henry failed to confirm his visit to Glen this year? He cannot – can he? – be contemplating another cruise on *The Enchantress* with Violet and – Margot pushes the thought from her mind – Venetia Stanley? He simply cannot be faithless enough to refuse Eddy, Margot's own brother – the source of so much of Mr Asquith's calm (for has not Eddy, like Sir Charles before him, contributed to the Asquith finances with splendid generosity: did not Mr Asquith make her brother a peer three years back?) – no, her Henry cannot possibly refuse to visit Scotland this year, and choose hot and unattractive places like Malta or Greece, when he could walk the hills of incomparable Glen. It is wondering about the Prime Ministerial indecision in the month of August that leads Margot to the conclusion that there will almost certainly be war.

Eddy is not in Scotland when Margot – for she is nothing if not impulsive – sends a telegram announcing her imminent arrival. He is in the South, so a tongue-tied Louisa says, stumbling over each word as Margot, picturing her in the basement at Glen by the telephone, sees glimpses of valley from the still-room window behind Louisa's shoulder and is overcome once more by the fierceness of her desire to be there. His Lordship, it turns out, is at Wilsford. He took Miss Clare and Master Bim down there – on the night train – but Margot, who lacks the patience to wonder at the wistful note so clearly audible in the maid-servant's voice at the mention of Bim's name, merely snaps out a question before ringing off. Her Ladyship? Yes, of course Pamela is at Wilsford also, and has been there all along. Pamela would never stay by choice at Glen.

So it is that Margot, small, formidable, ignoring those who give signs of recognition at Waterloo and staring angrily straight into the faces of those who do not, boards an early afternoon train to Salisbury; and, once settled in a first-class carriage, sits as ramrod-upright as an imported god, nose outlined in all its broken splendour (a hunting accident long ago: it has not prevented its owner from insisting on expensive dresses, usually from Worth, and the latest hats) and opens a newspaper, with the air of one who knows a good deal more than any editor on the subject of the coming war. A glance sideways as the train pulls out confirms her suspicion that the quiet, thoughtful fellow passenger who walks without haste down the corridor, looks into the compartment and bows in greeting is her husband's Foreign Secretary, Sir Edward Grey. The long-standing friendship between Grey and her brother Eddy – and the long love affair, so people say, between Grey and Eddy's wife Pamela – means that it is highly likely Grey will be a guest at Wilsford, too. Margot smiles back and immediately starts to pepper Grey with questions: is there any hope for Ireland? Is there anything she can do? She has some ideas, naturally, and would like to discuss them before they arrive and – here, lighting a cigarette inserted in the long cigarette holder, she appears by blowing out a plume of smoke to emit a magic signal to those who stand on the platform, and between Great Durnford and Amesbury, follows, his eyes already soft at the sight of Pamela in the doorway, the seven-year-old Stephen at her side. Her beauty, the simplicity of her white blouse and gathered dark skirt – the streak of mud on her cheek, planted by another son who runs up (David, or Kit perhaps, Grey's godson and champion of his mother to the last) – give an air of unpremeditated happiness, of full enjoyment at the spectacle presented by the children on the green. The old gypsy caravan, Margot notes with a dismissive tap of the cigarette holder, is out on the sward, proof of Pamela's tireless journeying on the downs with her 'jewels'. Clare, got up as a crusader, approaches with a smile. She kisses her aunt. Then, as Eddy walks from the oak door, 'old' as the rest of the manor, to greet his sister and his friend, the picture is complete. All that's needed now, Margot thinks sardonically, is a handful of the ghosts dear Pamela likes to claim she can summon up here. 'Isn't it remarkable?' Mrs Asquith has not been able to prevent herself from remarking on previous occasions to the assembled company, and in the presence of her sister-in-law, 'that people come from the other world to Wilsford, when they never were here before?' Margot's jests on the subject of Pamela's spiritualism have never gone down well – and as far as she is able to determine her own impulses, the Prime Minister's wife has promised herself she will desist from teasing Pamela on this visit to Wilsford. There is too much to think of, anyway: Margot must discuss politics with her brother, with Grey; must fill her diary; must walk all the way up the drove road to Stonehenge and rid herself – though she will not admit the proposed hard exercise is to be taken for this purpose – for ever of the horrid dreams.

The stone parlour at Wilsford, which opens out on to an expanse of lawn, this in turn widening and appearing to open to the clear, placid waters of the Avon, looks even further across the river, to a vista of water meadows, willows in a haze of grey-green, and gentle hills where Pamela likes to roam with the children. Here they are, in an earlier photograph, ladder extended from the sides of the gaily painted caravan: David, scowling, for he has just received a reprimand for stamping on a lark's nest, high on the downs; Kit, in the dark-blue knit Madeline Wyndham makes for all her grandchildren, a sailor already in his imagination; Bim, who likes to parade as a military man, gun at the ready – soon, prepared for war by all the tales of chivalry his mother reads him, and dressed as a soldier since he could walk, he will obey his uncle's summons and go off to war. And Clare (Stephen is too intent on himself, or on the affinity he finds with wild bee orchid or blue pimpernel, in the short grass up here, to face the camera: that will come later in life) – Clare, so beautiful she appears to belong more to river than air, standing sulky as ever, detached from the rest. Sir Oliver Lodge, the leading light in psychical research of the day, has expressed the hope that Pamela's lovely daughter will join the seances and hear the voices of the dead. But Clare is like her aunt Margot in her love of the world, even if she resembles her mother in beauty: she is wilful, spoiled already by her parents, and longs for the excitement of London, where she will behave badly and bring on herself little but misery and an air of petulance.

Pamela is in the stone parlour. Margot, whose first night of the visit has passed badly – no dreams, but she was woken by the sound of loud rapping, as if someone knocked on wood, impatiently – Margot has an unpleasant feeling that Pamela had decided to summon the dead in the night, to spite her worldly sister-in-law. After striding round the garden, oblivious to the prettiness of the pink-brown reeds, the bamboo-like Chinese brush-strokes in the pearly mist of the morning (she loves only Scotland, like her brother Eddy), she goes to the dining-room to discover the men; to talk. Pamela, who is making a paper hat for Stephen to set on his golden curls (why must she dress him as a girl? It must be time for the child to go to prep school at West Downs), shall remain in the stone parlour as long as she likes. Sir Edward Grey, who will stand for a time unseen at the door and regard her with helpless admiration, will come and take her away; they will go in search of birds: Pamela's white barn owl that flies along the old drove road by Springbottom Farm, under the downs that rise to Stonehenge; the larks and robins that Grey likes to tame, so they come and feed from his hand, perch even on his august head. Until then, the men are Margot's, in the dining-room where kedgeree and cold ham stand on hot plate and sideboard between the windows looking on the front garden, with its high steps and rose bower.

As Margot enters, Eddy slices the top from his hard-boiled egg and sprinkles on cayenne. He looks up at Margot and smiles, then as his eyes fill with concern, he pretends to have trouble scooping the egg and looks down again. Margot has become impossibly thin: why didn't he see it last night? For a moment Eddy wonders if all goes well with his sister and her life, then, as she begins to talk to him – of Ireland, of the coming war – and as Grey, glancing up in amusement from his chair nearest the window, the garden and the birds, tries to reply to his Prime Minister's wife, Eddy sits back, reassured again. Margot is Margot; she always will be; she is utterly self-sufficient, as she was in his youth and hers, riding and walking the moors at Glen. Nevertheless, Eddy can't help reflecting as he takes in his first mouthful of egg – for so mild a man, it has been remarked that cayenne pepper at breakfast is an unusual taste – that something has been worrying dear Margot lately. She is far too thin.

The morning doesn't proceed as Margot had expected. Eddy, for one, has an appointment to visit the cathedral, at Salisbury: doubtless, though he does not speak of it, money is to be bestowed for repair and upkeep; at one point, inheriting a sense of the nation's inheritance (from where no-one can say, for Eddy's fortune is as new as this manor house built of old stone on the site of a medieval nunnery), he owns ruined abbeys in Scotland, has a sacrificial slab of Stonehenge and opens the old Bart's picture collection to the public in his house at Queen Anne's Gate. Sir Charles's collection, of Reynolds, Gainsborough, Bonington, Raeburn, is on show there. The entrance fee is donated to charity. Eddy, a space-age away from the bleach works in Glasgow as he sits over breakfast in the Wiltshire Downs, is the perfect gentleman. When Bim (how tall and handsome he has grown!) comes in to say Mummy is ready, will they take the victoria into Salisbury? – she is sure it will not rain – it's possible even for the most cynical (and Margot knows the children of the Souls, given the appellation The Coterie, are famed for their sense of irony and their cynicism) to say that Eddy and all he stands for are worth fighting for in the coming war.

Not that the war will be such a long-drawn-out affair. As Eddy, bunching his napkin, throws it on the table (for Eddy has discovered, along with the necessity of dispensing charity, that he need not be neat in his habits: out of all the family, only Kit learns to be tidy and clean, at Dartmouth Naval College) and leaves to go in search of Pamela, who waits now in the front hall, family bible in hand, their son Bim, their hope and their joy, expresses his opinion of the approaching fray.

'Oh, Aunt Margot, it will all be over by Christmas,' Bim says – for Margot, unable to resist this opportunity to corner Edward Grey and extract information from him, has inevitably brought up the subject of Germany, Belgium and France. 'Won't it, sir?' Bim presses Grey – who has half-risen as Pamela waves goodbye from the hall. Bim has the eagerness of a young sportsman anticipating a polo match. But Margot has already noticed Pamela's change of attitude to her son going off to war. Where once she had spoken only of peace, now – as if death lies in the faint outline of garden where it merges with rushes and reedbeds, and the deep cuts, almost waterless at this time of year, are like scars in the perilous land between lawn and river bank – she accepts the necessity of her son's sacrifice when the time comes. If Bim sees and accepts it, too, he gives no sign.

Margot and Grey walk the steep, unmade road up to the downs, Eddy's unsuitable conifers in a tall line blocking the view of the sweep of the land. Margot walks at a furious pace, head down as if a wind would attack at any time, though the late July day is in fact muggy and windless. Sir Edward, no longer able to parry the questions she fires at him, stops out of breath at the crest of the hill. They gaze down at Springbottom Farm, where the old drove road from the Stones ends and the lane over to Wilsford rises in a tangle of dogwood and wild rose. 'I have made a proposal,' Grey says. He glances at Margot; regrets the absence of Pamela, and the quiet walk they would have enjoyed. Even the swallows, which nest in the eaves of the farm every year, have made great loops of inky black against the sky as they fly from Margot's piercing tones and assertive manner. When Pamela walks there, the birds circle her head before dipping in and out of nests high in the old farmhouse's crumbling brick. 'I have proposed to Germany, France and Italy that a conference with Great Britain take place at the earliest possible opportunity.'

'Ah.' Margot shows her satisfaction at obtaining news from the source she most respects next to her husband, by turning to face Grey. She sees the downs empty and bare, without a telegraph pole or a vehicle in sight. Her pulse throbs; she stands still, waiting for more.

'No reply has been received from Germany,' Grey says simply. He attempts to add some words, as Margot now turns again, away from the landscape of ancient grazing land, tumuli that stick up on the horizon, from under the quilting of grass, like hot-water bottles in beds. Margot begins to walk back down to Wilsford, to the house, to urgency and telegrams. 'I inform the House tomorrow,' Grey says, but by now he is unsure whether Margot can hear him. Already the small, jerky figure is at the foot of the lane; it crosses the road to the churchyard and cuts through Pamela's mock village to the cobbled stableyard and the back door. A surprised Louis Ford stands back as she marches in. Sir Edward sighs and walks round to the front of the manor. Something in him knows it will be a long time before the woman who will one day be his wife (who will marry him when Eddy dies) returns from the visit to Salisbury. He is prepared to wait. Red boxes stand in the hall; and Nanny Trusler, hurrying through in search of the youngest, Stephen, in order to brush his hair before lunch, murmurs in apology. Grey sits down and decides to light a cigarette before opening a red box. There is not really so long to wait – for Pamela, or for war.

It's Wednesday, 29th July. Margot lies on her bed at No. 10 Downing Street. It's the hour for her rest before dinner, but she cannot sleep: the hooting of horns outside, the cries of street traffic, the screams of trains keep her wakeful and anxious. The louder the sound, the worse her headache becomes, until she has the sensation she is wrapped in thick muslin, pain coming through with the persistence of muffled drums. Fear of war has taken away all her vitality: only the sound of Henry's step, only the arrival of the foreign telegrams in response to Grey's initiative will clear her mind, set her upright again. But nothing comes. Mr Asquith sits hunched over the composition of a letter to Venetia Stanley (so Margot imagines and she is almost certainly right). Margot's daughter Elizabeth, summoned to return from Holland immediately, is not expected till this evening. In her half-conscious state, Margot remembers the incredulity of the luncheon guests at the recall of Elizabeth, along with Margot's pronouncement that she has also put a stop on her sister Lucy's proposed painting trip to France. Neither the Archbishop of Canterbury nor Lord d'Abernon appeared to believe that there is any threat of war whatsoever; the rare occasions of Margot's return of energy come with her indignation at this. Silly old fools! If they knew what Margot knows (she has confronted her husband on return from Wiltshire, and he has told her all – at last!), then they'd take another line altogether. Margot has claimed to understand men who love stamps and stones – but she cannot understand men who love war. She has a sneaking feeling the luncheon guests may fall into this latter category, and that is why they pretend to refuse the possibility of the horrors that are to come. Don't all men – with the exception of dear Henry, of course – secretly long to go to war?

The last part of Margot's visit to Eddy and Pamela ended in hostility, as Margot had feared all along it would. She shuts off the memory of Sunday afternoon in the stone parlour and of the visit of Sir Oliver Lodge from his house nearby, and the ensuing conversation about psychic phenomena. How can Edward Grey stand this sort of nonsense? He is the most rational of men. For that matter, how can Margot's own brother Eddy be on the brink of converting to this belief in the spirit world? It's almost as if he fears something so intensely that the table-turning and tapping are used as a prophylactic – but against what? Margot also fears she knows the answer to this, but she doesn't dare admit it, especially now, when the fate of the Western world hangs by a thread. Eddy surely fears for his son, for open-hearted Bim, who in his attempt to reach out to the world goes into the street from the door of his parents' house in London and asks any passer-by in to share his dinner. Eddy, like Pamela, must see Bim already on the battlefield, dead.

None of this had been able to curb Margot's waspish tongue. Come an opening – Pamela, eyes down under sculpted lids, talking of messages received from the other world – and the wife of the Prime Minister is in with a *bon mot* (it's not the first time she's delivered it, either). 'It can be said of someone that they're not making any sense,' says Margot – and Pamela looks across apprehensively as her sister-in-law tips ash from the long holder into the blue and white porcelain plate on the oak table, where Pamela and Stephen make dresses and cut out patterns for his dolls. 'But it's nothing to the rubbish the dead talk!' Silence all round, of course. Finally, Edward Grey gets to his feet and suggests to Pamela that they go for a walk down to the weir. As the party disperses, the roar of the distant water can be heard, and the screech of peacocks from the garden at Lake House above the weir pool. Margot, remembering, turns in her bed so that the pillow goes right over her face.

For all her sense of impending doom, it is the nearness of catastrophe that will save Margot's marriage, along with her self-esteem – for even Henry and his infatuation cannot deny that the wife of the Prime Minister must be informed when war is inevitable. Doom hangs in the passages, and haunts the dinner menu Margot has to sit up at her desk to write out, for the following evening, Thursday, 30th July. 'Quails' Eggs in Aspic,' she writes on a blank sheet of paper white as the PM's face, as he opens the door silently into the bedroom he so seldom enters these days, and stands irresolute there; 'Consommé; Crown of Lamb'. On a facing sheet she begins the guest list: Winston Churchill (now in charge of the Admiralty, longing for the coming conflagration as much as Margot dreads it); Violet Asquith – and here Margot's hand quivers a little – next to her father at table (she'd insist, anyway), and on the other side, Rupert Brooke.

It is 7.30 in the evening: as soon as Margot sees her husband standing there she knows that doom is about to be succeeded by the sentence of death. She sits back in her chair, expecting him to pace the room, as he has always done when spelling out the latest news to her. But now he stands quite still and, for the first time in what seems an age, they look at each other.

Mr Asquith announces he has sent the precautionary telegram to every part of the Empire, that they must prepare for war, and Margot stares still into her husband's face. She sees there defeat, tiredness, and the calm for which she loves him – though she has come to wish that calm buried in anguish for a return of her love this past year. She thinks he loves her; she thinks of money, of the £5,000 a year settled by the old Bart on his most outspoken daughter; of the support Henry has received from her family and herself; of the coming back of the old ways, now he has visited her in her bedroom to tell her the world is indeed doomed to die.

Margot writes later: 'Deeply moved and thrilled with excitement, I observed the emotion in his face and said: "Has it come to this?" At which he nodded without speaking, and after kissing me left the room.'

Margot's power is restored to her at last – at the House of Commons, where the 'ugly pretty stupid clever West End ladies' crowd round her in the Gallery, calling for news, expressing horror at the putting off of the Irish Amending Bill, which had been awaited with passionate excitement and was to have taken place that day: 'We are on the verge of a European war,' says Margot, as she sweeps past, *en route* to her husband's room. At dinner the next evening, the quails' eggs are washed down by the champagne which the fortune of the hostess provides, and, by placing the handsome young poet Rupert Brooke opposite Winston Churchill, she prompts him to offer his services to the Royal Naval Division, a new military unit under the administration of the Admiralty. Thanks to Margot, with the help of Churchill's private secretary Eddy Marsh, Brooke will be in uniform soon, along with the Prime Minister's son, Oc Asquith. Better still, Margot's letter, written two days later than this, to the Irish Secretary John Redmond, is more successful than she had dared to hope. The 'line' to Mr Redmond, in which she assures him he will set an 'unforgettable example' if he would go to the Commons on Monday and in a great speech offer all his soldiers to the Government, receives a reply from him, saying he hopes he 'may be able to follow your advice'.

Margot begins to eat better, and to spend less time in her room, bent over her writing-desk. But, for all the resumption of control, which uplifts her, she hates the war and those who love it – and when the midnight deadline on Monday, 3rd August has passed, and Grey, despondent after a dinner in which every subject was dropped as soon as it was picked up, has finally gone back to the Foreign Office to declare the future, to make his famous statement about the lamps going out all over Europe, Margot confides to her diary, after a night without peace or rest, 'Too exhausted to think, I lay sleepless in bed. Bursts of cheering broke like rockets in a silent sky, and I listened to snatches of "God Save the King" shouted in front of the Palace all through the night.'

THREE

Hester and Clare

Clare Tennant, 1917

The year of dead children. Hester, Pamela's longed-for second daughter, one day old, awaits the photographer with the resignation and sweetness of death. She is a harbinger of the tragedies that follow, as the heather comes stubbornly to purple in August 1916 and blazes right through that fateful September in the Somme. Mourning, Pamela stands as white as a cross against the northern sky. Margot, believed indifferent by her sister-in-law to the fall of Mr Asquith's son Raymond, and to the death of her own nephew Bim, vents her anguish in the pages of her diary. But there is too much sorrow everywhere for the pain of Mr Asquith's wife to be taken seriously. Margot's own son is not old enough to be sent to the Front: let her send her condolences to Pamela's sister, Mary Wemyss, who has lost two sons, and to Ettie Desborough – who is 'wonderful' after the cruel loss of her brilliant son Julian and his brother Billy. Let Margot sneer as she may at the Other World, peopled now by the men who walked towards the German machine-guns. For, whatever the much-castigated Mrs Asquith may think, the dead are talking, sending messages through books in the libraries of their wealthy owners. (How can the poor communicate, Margot wonders, still rebellious when faced with this new religion, if they do not possess a full set of Matthew Arnold?)

The lost sons crowd the meadows of Wilsford and the Oriel window at Stanway, where Pamela's sister

Mary looks up and sees their faces in ancient glass lit by the sun. Bim – who belongs more to the maid Louisa in death than ever he could in life (she is brought up to the room at Glen painted with dogs and foxes, the room known as The Kennels, for seances with Pamela, who claims she has discovered psychic powers in the girl) – Bim lives, in his loving references to Eddy's trees, and to his darling mother most of all.

Pamela, living with the dead, with the pale face of Hester, for whom she invents a life as romantic as that of her own great-grandmother, the first Pamela, fills her white vellum-bound books, her tombstones to the son and daughter who now will never know each other. A tide of sentiment sweeps the nation: just as Margot is hissed off the stage, Pamela is admired, her books read, her medium Mrs Leonard – an account of her renowned 'book tests' appears in Pamela's *The Earthen Vessel* – sought-after and consulted by all the great families decimated by their terrible loss. Bim's poem 'Home Thoughts from Laventie' is published. Rupert Brooke will continue the tradition. Stranded in the graveyard of their world, mothers and fathers of the marvellous boys read of vanished Aprils and halted clocks and see nothing but the extinction of all hope.

To make matters worse, Clare has given birth to a living daughter in this year of grief. Louisa, imported to Wilsford so that she can summon up the spirits in the place close to Pamela's – and to Bim's – heart, can feel her mistress's wish to evade her daughter and new granddaughter: why must they come and stay all the time, when Pamela wants only to be alone with her ghosts? Even in London, at 34 Queen Anne's Gate, Clare insists on coming to stay. The ménage leaves Wilsford for London tomorrow, Mrs Leonard has recommended the library in Eddy's house as a fine source for Bim's latest message from beyond. Can it be, Louisa wonders pragmatically, that young Miss Clare (now a married woman, of course, but it's hard to see her that way) wants to dump her baby on her mother? It doesn't take a psychic to understand that if this is indeed the case, then the idea isn't going down well at all.

It's their last day at Wilsford before going into Salisbury to take the train up to town. Pamela, who has written a poem for Hester in which the child, half-spirit, has all her tastes in flowers, landscape and mood dictated by her mother (so much more convenient than coming up against real children, David thinks as he watches the 'darling moth' of his adored elder brother Bim wander the meadows, summoning the daughter who is obedient, because she is dead) – Pamela, walking on a blowy day with leaves scuttling about the Round House, to the river, stops there looking out.

A boy is coming downstream in a punt. She knows him, she doesn't remember who he is, but he is certainly from the village, from Amesbury: didn't a letter of condolence come only last week, reminding her of the chops and steaks she used to grill here at the Round House, the miniature thatched rotunda built for the children, hidden in trees beyond her village green? Bim, the letter said, so much enjoyed those meals when the village came ... As Pamela stands, and feels the full weight of her grief, the punt comes in to the muddy bank; the child, about nine years old, is hopelessly stuck there; and Stephen, displaced by his dead sister but determined to grab back that demanding, stifling love, runs down between the high yew hedges to take hold of his mother's hand.

Truly, Pamela cannot say why or how she took the boy as one of hers. An old woman in Amesbury remembered the lady coming and saying she'd lost a child: can she have this one? Stephen, gazing in disbelief at the rat's tails of the lad who scrambles ashore, shakes his golden hair in response to this river-steeped urchin climbing out towards them through dead osier-beds and over a well of beech leaves, perilous to the tread.

'Oliver!' says Pamela, whether the lad's name is Oliver or not. And she looks solemnly across at Stephen: her expression assures him of her love; Hester, like the soft September wind, has died down in the branches of the trees. Pamela takes Stephen's hair, a skein of spun silk that runs through her fingers as she speaks to the village boy. They will all be friends now, won't they? She will go and find his family – wouldn't he like to live here, at the manor, and go fishing with the other boys down at the weir?

And Stephen will be his friend for ever – will he give his word on it now?

Louisa, watching as she always does – when at Glen, from a high turret window, or here at Wilsford, from below the eaves of the 'old' thatched nursery wing, which sticks right out into the garden and affords a view of vegetables and fruit trees, and the fringe of reeds at the base of Wilsford's sloping land – wonders at the embrace her mistress gives to the dirty village boy. She'll have to wash his clothes, she sees that, when the nature of this strange adoption becomes clear. More work; but Louisa, since the death of Bim, has grown in stature in Pamela's household, and already names Connie the under-housemaid as the one who will be responsible for Pamela's latest whim. Louisa, more even than the 'hell-kittens' who had been friends of Bim (thus named by Pamela, even though she saw no challenge to her absolute supremacy in the heart of her son), is queen of the spirit world, accepted by Mrs Leonard as a seer of quite extraordinary power. The Scotch maid, despite the fact she is incapable of doing the book test – for she can write her name and nothing else, and most certainly cannot read – has nevertheless produced Bim for Her Ladyship in the most convincing manner. On occasions when Edward Grey and Pamela's husband Eddy, too polite to complain, wait downstairs in the drawing-room at 34 Queen Anne's Gate and the thumping and tapping overhead become quite impossible to ignore, Louisa has demonstrated her unusual gifts. Osbert Sitwell is so much in awe of her that he fears a visit to Wilsford: the tapping keeps him awake all night.

This orphan from Amesbury will be no threat to Louisa – and will not even, as is plain to see, take Pamela's mind for long from Bim and from the poem of Hester. The kind words written to her on the subject of her art by her eldest son as he lay in the trenches, awaiting orders to go over the top, are no more than Pamela expected. Even with the approach of death, Bim had expressed anxiety that his mother was not with the right publisher. Now the question will be – as Louisa, whose eye can look as accurately into the future as it purportedly can into the world of dead sons, says caustically to Mrs Ford, all agog in the shiny-painted kitchen at the back of the manor – the question will be the future of the lad when he's a grown man. And it takes Mrs Ford, who has always nurtured a soft spot for Stephen, to say that the boy from Amesbury needn't expect much kindness from Miss Clare or Master David; but Christopher – Kit – how tall and bronzed he was, when he came back off the *Lord Nelson* and tried to reassure them all at home that there would soon be an end to this terrible war; and even young Stephen himself – selfish though you might consider him to be – he had it in him to look after the poor lad when he's a man. But Louisa replies that the wretch is as likely as not to be sent off to sea as soon as Her Ladyship tires of him; and he can count himself lucky if Master Stephen sends him so much as a pinch of snuff. Mrs Ford is silent: Louis has bustled into the kitchen to say the victoria is ready: he's at sixes and sevens, is Her Ladyship taking the village lad to London, or leaving him here?

Louisa, recalled to her duties as clairvoyant, says grandly that it would not do at all for the boy to travel on the train with the family. And as she speaks, her eyes shine: for soon, in the darkened first-floor room at 34 Queen Anne's Gate, and in the company of two hand-picked hell-kittens, Ava and Cynthia by name, her Bim will rejoin the company.

* * *

Clare is indeed at home when her mother and entourage arrive. For a moment Pamela's gaze softens: how beautiful Clare is! How she resembles her mother: wasn't the *tableau vivant*, when Clare outshone the lovely Lady Diana Manners, choosing a painting by Raphael rather than Lady Diana's 'idea of a Tiepolo' to pose for the awe-struck audience, the greatest compliment to the looks Pamela knows she has inherited from the daughter of Philippe Egalité, the cousin of Louis XVI of France? For Pamela and her brother George always insisted they were the 'French' ones of the family, and who dared contradict them? (Mrs Belloc Lowndes, a toady in the view of the acerbic Margot, helps disseminate this myth, which enthrals all those who hear of the well-born wife of a wealthy man adopting Rousseauesque principles and choosing to care more for her children than for the worldly pleasures of London society.) But Margot, refraining from employing on her sister-in-law her epithet on Lady Desborough, that she tells 'enough white lies to ice a cake', is nevertheless unable to resist a dig or two on the subject of Pamela's annual expenditure. Her sister-in-law's 'simple' life doesn't convince. That Margot is herself known to be addicted to prising dresses, trinkets and pictures from friends and strangers alike makes no difference to the Prime Minister's wife. 'Money!' Margot has been known to exclaim. 'It means no more to me than almonds and raisins!'

Clare is not holding her baby daughter: Nanny Trusler, stiff with disapproval, is caring for the child in the upstairs nursery. (But Stephen will need his tea, as he's just off the train; and of course Pamela has decided after all to bring the new addition to the family, the child she has named Oliver, to London. 'Nanny, Oliver will need a shirt and shoes and – you do it, Nanny, please!') Maybe what annoys Pamela is that her own voice, so cajoling, so reasonable in its demands, as if an equal is being asked to perform an act by another, has been fiendishly copied by Clare. Her daughter does indeed resemble her – and Eddy, who has pandered to his eldest child since she was the age of her own baby now, will not see that it is far from reasonable of Clare to expect the attention of everyone at Queen Anne's Gate whenever she feels like it. Why, thinks Pamela – whose face darkens, the obstinate jaw-line preparing for a long silence, her face in profile unlike the adoring visage of a mother with whom the children have from an early age learned to 'preparate' in expectation of a photographer or a lover coming to the door – why doesn't Clare go back to her husband in the country? Handsome – a soldier – even if he is not actually in the shires at the moment, but is instead crouching in the mud of battle, his land, his house – most of all, his old nursery – is where Clare and her daughter belong. 'Have you heard from Adrian?' Pamela enquires icily of her daughter.

Of course, everyone, even Pamela, knows the answer. As Clare dances every night in Ciros, or in the houses in Curzon Street or at Arlington House or beyond; as she runs to the summer picnics with her basket of ham and eggs in jelly from Jermyn Street, wine from the cellar of a house where the brave young son may never come back; as Clare falls through the front door of home, exhausted, hollow-cheeked, burning-eyed from the ragtime, the parties where black musicians play their rhythms to the sound of chatter on the stairs, and excited whispering in parlours and bedrooms, so her husband the gallant Captain writes from the trenches and dreams of the wife with whom he has fallen so desperately in love.

In her own flat – but Clare prefers it here, it's so central and Nanny Trusler is on hand, even if Pamela's habit of wandering around the picture gallery at Queen Anne's Gate speaking to the portraits does drive her to distraction – in her two rooms in Mayfair, Clare has quite lost the habit of opening her husband's letters. They pile up in the hall as she dances – always with the same man nowadays, the best dancer in London, that's how he is known. Lionel, the handsomest cricketer in the land, who will go on to be Captain of England after the war. The other Captain, the dim husband, is forgotten and might as well, along with so many others in this time of sad revelry, be dead.

So Clare doesn't reply to her mother's enquiry; she has ammunition in the ragged child she saw led to the back stairs by Louisa a moment ago and decides to use it now. (At the same time, she fears the effect of the deaths of Hester and of Bim, as if Pamela, carrying her own death within her and that of her children, might lapse into a decline from which there would be no awakening. Clare needs her mother still: jealousy of her dead sister makes her competitive, edgy: she wants Pamela alive, that she may exact some love from her, at last.)

'That boy you brought with you is the child caught stealing, on the day we went up to Imber, on the downs,' says Clare triumphantly, all the same. 'We were in the caravan, we returned and caught him red-handed – surely, Mummy, you remember that?'

This time Clare has gone too far. She sees it as soon as she's spoken: she feels the whiteness and stiffness in the room, as if a sea wave had risen there, solidified, scattered into granules of ice. Clare seldom feels, or sees, these things – the new colours that invade London, as if the future must march ahead whether the war would have it or not; the dances, the paintings of a terrifying modernism leave her unmoved and unaware. Clare's soul will dwell for ever in the Ritz dining-room, with its gilt and decorative ceiling, and the deep curtains that hide the passing poor on the pavements outside. She is not sensitive to mood, to colour or light. But today, now – as Stephen dances into the room, nine years old, and for the first time sees his sister's beauty and falls silent in envy and a desire to match it himself one day – now, Clare feels her mother's hatred and falls silent, while her brain races ahead to the evening's fun. The Café Royal is where Lionel has suggested they meet. Who cares if all the world knows that the wayward daughter of Pamela and Eddy is flaunting a romance with the famous cricketer? Even if her aunt Margot, who has dismissed Clare's lover, grandson of the poet Alfred Tennyson, as 'uncouth', has spoken crossly to her, on the last occasion of a meeting at a dress show in Downing Street, what can she or anyone do to stop the course of true love? Isn't Mr Asquith himself known to be heartbroken at the marriage of his Venetia a year ago – who is the beak-nosed aunt to criticise now? She doesn't know about love, that's clear. She has even spoken to Eddy, who worries that his daughter will run through all her money. Lionel is known for his penury and his extravagant tastes.

Pamela stands as silent as her daughter and away from her, so she can look down the street and see Edward Grey come up from Birdcage Walk. An hour without the cares of the Foreign Office – no matter if today there is a seance planned and the Foreign Secretary must wait. He has troubles enough, in this war which has taken seven young men from Eddy's family and as many again from Pamela's own; she sees him, as he walks elegantly along, in the guise of a figure painted in brush-strokes on a Cretan vase: the Minotaur of War lurks in the labyrinth as he weaves his way through cab horses and motor cars to the woman he loves. Pamela's thoughts are far, as ever, from her daughter Clare.

Doors bang. Louisa, pulling on the orphan boy's new trousers (discarded by Stephen a year ago: they don't fit him, he complained, though that was demonstrably untrue), swears at the disappearance of Connie, the second housemaid. Not everyone is as impressed by Louisa's new status as Her Ladyship is – and His Lordship, too, has personally congratulated Louisa on her summoning of poor Bim's aura from the lilac wastes of the world where the young soldiers have all 'gone on'. Connie, for one, has sniffed and pointed out that Louisa must look after the washing, clear the tea things and clean up after Master David when he's not at school. Master Christopher – won't he be the new Lord one day, now Bim is dead? – is a pleasure to look after, of course: Connie reserves for herself the quick whisk-round in the bleak room where Kit folds his sheets on top of his eiderdown and leaves his silver hair-brushes, gifts from his godfather Edward Grey, in a neat arrangement on the top of the chest of drawers. It occurs to her – but she doesn't say so to Louisa – that his mother hasn't taken in yet that this second son should move from his cell-like quarters at Queen Anne's Gate, Wilsford and Glen. He is the heir and Connie has overheard a conversation, when down in the old manor, between Pamela and a gentleman who comes to see her as often as he is permitted, all the way from Somerset. He's in love with Pamela, like all the rest. He has a daughter, also named Pamela – Connie does allow Louisa to know that this young Pamela has been booked, as it were, for Christopher one day. 'They'll make a lovely couple.' The girl sighs, and knows her fatuous remark has gone unheard – for all his good looks, and his narrow escape from death on the beaches of Gallipoli, the second son interests Louisa no more than he does his mother.

More doors bang – Clare is leaving now: Louisa, after struggling with Oliver's shoes, straightens up and looks down into the street, where Clare and her mother's lover pass each other on the doorstep. A cab is hailed; but from it, before Clare can sail off to her flat, her own lover, and the pile of unopened letters in the hall from poor Adrian, spill girls as bright and ephemeral as scarves: their voices sound all the way up the outside of the house. They kiss Clare, dash into 34 Queen Anne's Gate and past the gallery where the lace-ribboned Reynolds and Gainsborough actresses and noblewomen hang. They are the present, they have nothing to do with the powdered ladies of the past: their hair is tied back in great bows; they are Flappers; and all Louisa can do, as she goes with her new, gliding step (but she is clumsy still: a bust of Herodotus trembles on its plinth as she brushes it with an elbow awkwardly aslant), is know herself, for all her supernatural powers, an unbridgeable world away from Miss Ava and Miss Cynthia, their pearls and money – and, most unattainable of all, their ability to seize a pen, to write the jet-rimmed letters of condolence that have drawn them to Pamela and right into her heart.

The library is hushed and still. A faint smell of cigar smoke hangs in the room. Louisa stands by the writing-table, where Pamela's white vellum journal lies open. She cannot read the words, in the well-behaved handwriting, but she knows the little book received its first entry shortly after the massacre of the Somme: 'The news reached us on Tuesday, 17th September. Edward was by his writing-table, I was reading my letters in the armchair in the library. He came across to me and I read it in his face. "Has the news come?" I asked. "It is come," he said.'

Louisa knows these words by heart because she has caused David – frequently roped in for seances, though he will embrace the conspicuous consumption of the modern world when it comes at the end of the war: a Tiger Moth plane; a Hispano Suiza in the stables at Wilsford; pyjama parties; a refusal of the Soul (possibly this commodity did indeed disappear in the aftermath of the war) – Louisa has caused David to read passages from the journal aloud to her. In exchange for a pinch on the bottom and a promise to come up to his room when 'Moth' is down in the country, he does so.

So Louisa knows several of the entries in this most secret of journals by heart. She knows Pamela's sad dream, when Bim comes to her and she can feel 'the grip of his embrace around me' (here Louisa closes her eyes, the better to feel it too) 'and see the wonderfully tender expression in his eyes. He had the mud of the battlefield on his khaki, but his face looked quite rested.' At this point, Louisa breaks down and cries.

There's no time for a reading of Pamela's confidences today: Mrs Leonard the medium must have arrived while the girl stood there dreaming. Ava and Cynthia, always identifiable from the tapping of their tiny feet in exquisite shoes, a sound both suggestive of a geisha obedience and of a strong expectation of always getting their way, are coming down the passage with the force of a hailstorm. Pamela's voice can be heard, calling out to Stephen, 'I am going to wear my butterfly brooch today, because it is Earth, and a butterfly means Psyche – the Soul.' And Louisa sighs. She's almost sorry for the vain, effeminate boy.

As the curtains are drawn across, and the round table begins to move at the prompting of Mrs Leonard, whose clay-vessel-shaped face looms over the proceedings like a dim light bulb, which only serves to illumine the sense of utter darkness in which all are plunged, Louisa feels her power return to her and the table rears and then runs all the way from B to I as if engaged in a steeplechase. 'It's Bim, come back when Louisa asks him,' whispers Pamela happily.

Downstairs Sir Edward Grey, newspaper stretched out before him, observes a pigeon as it crash-lands on the balustrade of the terrace that runs along the garden at Queen Anne's Gate. The bird, with its bright eyes and ruff of iridescent green, looks in at him. But today – he cannot say why, but he's tired, tired of the war and of loving Pamela – the Foreign Secretary doesn't go in search of bread in the kitchens. He stares back at the bird; a thump from the room overhead makes his temples throb; and he rises, to go and open the french windows on to the stone terrace there. With a loud, disappointed sound, the bird flies away and settles in an elm. Grey watches it waddle along the twisted branches; then turns, with an effort, to greet Pamela's husband Eddy as he comes in.

Louisa is in her element, just ten feet above the Foreign Secretary's head. Even Mrs Leonard, whose book tests mean so much to the bereaved mothers who seek her out, is eclipsed by the Scotch maid's prescience and new, articulate manner of speech. 'Bim is laying his hand on your brooch,' Louisa says in a loud, clear voice. 'He says he knows why you put it on.' Pamela's eyes are glistening; Ava and Cynthia, who are scared and excited but also want to get to the Ritz for lunch, exchange glances and make secret vows to invite themselves to Glen next month: it's fun when the pheasant-shooting season opens and there are fewer seances in The Kennels, the frightening high-up room guarded by a dead boar's head.

'Who gave me the brooch?' says Pamela in a sad, shaky voice. 'Ask dear Bim if he can possibly remember, dear.'

Eddy, politely putting aside on his table in the study the sheets that estimate income for the profligate Clare, chats amicably with Edward Grey and they arrange to go up to Fallodon together. Fallodon in Northumberland is Sir Edward's home. Eddy knows, without of course it ever being mentioned, that his wife will marry Grey and live there, should anything happen to him. He and the other Edward are already seen as Pamela's two husbands: sometimes he thinks it wouldn't matter at all if he simply slipped away.

'Yes, his grandfather gave it to me,' cries Pamela, in the room above her spouses present and future, her thoughts only on the presence of her eldest son. 'But – I ask you all – how could Bim have remembered that? He was only two or three years old at the time.'

The table heaves and runs. At 10 Downing Street, where Margot is opening her letters in the morning-room, Mr Asquith looks in on his way to the club. Margot has complained to him recently on several occasions about the behaviour of Clare, and he was even prevailed upon to write to the uncouth bounder with whom his wife's niece is seen day and night. It's a scandal to the family. But today Mr Asquith regrets, as so often before, that he was coerced by Margot into approaching the unprepossessing young man – even if he is a famous cricketer. If Clare and Lionel love each other – well, there is such a thing as divorce. The only pity is that Venetia's defection into marriage with Edwin Montagu last year, just when a coalition Government threatened and the Prime Minister was at his lowest for years, should show so few signs of ending that way.

In Queen Anne's Gate, as Louisa spells out the letters which the table grunts and rolls to reach, and Eddy passes the Glen game book to Grey – he's particularly proud of this year's bag, the grouse are plentiful despite the war – Margot in Downing Street eyes her husband and sees that he is less calm, his features more animated with anger than they usually are. 'What is it, Henry?' demands Margot. She fears the loss of power of the Prime Minister: cruel people are saying she'd do anything to keep him in office. (And, of course, they gossip slanderously, 'The governess at Downing Street is German. Didn't you know? Margot and her daughter Elizabeth are very close to the Germans.' Margot is hated, but she gives no sign that she listens or cares.)

AT TATAR, the table at Queen Anne's Gate finally spells out. Pamela gives a little shriek. Mrs Leonard, outdone by the crude kennels girl from Scotland, goes over to the windows and pulls the curtains back. A sunny, early autumn day shows itself: Cynthia and Ava envisage Green Park after luncheon and the attention of anyone who is not dragooned to go off to this voracious war – or, as is the case with so many of their friends and cousins, is not already dead.

'It was Bim's name for his grandfather,' Pamela is saying, as the kindness of the autumn sunlight fills the library, settles on the little vellum book where she will record all this and lends it a golden patina. 'Only he could have known . . . When he was two or three years old . . . Attatar. Why, I'd quite forgotten it myself.'

The table is moved to the corner of the room; downstairs both Eddy and Sir Edward listen to the familiar sound of legs with claw feet being dragged over the parquet. Both, with different pretexts, rise and wander out into the hall. Ava and Cynthia, as they lead her downstairs, are kissing the devastated, radiant Pamela.

'This is the reply to my letter the scoundrel had the infernal cheek to send me,' says Mr Asquith, advancing on his wife in Downing Street and holding out an envelope – from which, whether she wishes to or not, Margot must extract the letter from Lionel within.

'Dear Mr Asquith,' Margot reads, and as she bends her head to the offending page her nose seems to dip to meet her chin, so that her husband, dreaming still of Venetia's sweetness and youth, thinks savagely that Margot could beat the man who tries to run off with her niece any time: she's Mr Punch today and should have looked after the misdemeanours of her own family instead of calling on him.

Margot is so impassioned with rage that she has to read the one-line letter again: 'Dear Mr Asquith' – the words dance before her eyes – 'You are an interfering old buger [*sic*].'

And it's signed by Lionel. Does he have no shame?

FOUR

Stephen

Stephen Tennant, 1926

Stephen sits at his drawing-board in what was once the stone parlour at Wilsford. It's September 1925; he is eighteen years old; the promise of beauty has been fulfilled; and as he sketches the bridesmaids' dresses for his elder brother Christopher's wedding, a camera records the concave cheeks (Stephen has been ill lately, but the family TB has lent a slenderness, a brilliance to the eye). The photographer on this occasion is only poor Louis Ford, who has been told not to fidget while he is arranging the tripod: the days of Cecil Beaton are a year or so away; but, like the snakes and lizards with which the new young master of Wilsford Manor has filled his 'reptillery', Stephen lies in wait for his prey – in his case, the glory and glamour of publicity.

Nanny Trusler is never far from Stephen – for all the sophistication of the young man, already praised for his drawings and poems, already (far too soon, in Nanny Trusler's opinion) the star of an exhibition in London of his art, the lonely, precocious child is still in need of his nurse. With Eddy dead four years back, and Lady Grey – as she now is – spending so much of her time at Fallodon, her husband's Northumberland home, Stephen is more in need of Nanny Trusler than ever. For one thing, her basilisk stare can be counted on to frighten away the bores who come flocking to Wilsford, expecting the pious, 'simple' way of life that Stephen's mother had instigated there. Nanny, with the backing of Louis and Mrs Ford, repels spiritualists, kindly neighbours and visiting relatives alike: No, Mr Stephen is not at home. But they can all see him, through a chink in the tall hedge, which once had shielded the ancient nunnery. Stephen in his parrot house, where the birds fly from his shoulder to perch on Bright Young Things welcome to partake of this most artificial and temporary of hospitalities. Stephen at an upper window, dressed in gold and silver lamé – well, it gives them something to talk about, Stephen says to Nanny Trusler, when she remonstrates that 'Cousin Nan' has come all the way from London to catch a glimpse of Eddy's most unexpected son. Uncle Jack and Uncle Frank: Stephen doesn't like to be reminded of his father's side of the family. Pamela's roots of course are different; and through her come the kind of people with whom Stephen feels he can associate. Lord Alfred Douglas, the 'Bosie' who was the ruin of Oscar Wilde, is, after all, Pamela's first cousin. Even if Stephen agrees with his mother that Bosie was dreadful to barge in on one of her great Liberal political evenings and shout obscenities at Robbie Ross, Stephen knows the value of the newspaper farrago that followed the otherwise dull and worthy event. It's only a matter of months before he, the most glittering and outrageous product of the aftermath of his uncle's Armageddon, hits the headlines himself, with a succession of parties – and, later, a love affair with Siegfried Sassoon. Stephen will reign over a world fringed with silver palm trees, set out seductively with limed and whitened furniture, bleached and stripped so that no trace of an Edwardian or Victorian past can survive.

Pamela is, it goes without saying, obstinately

present in Stephen's new décor (an 'old' manor house made modern, an irony that does not escape the acerbic Clare, and which will, after the death of their mother, grow increasingly bizarre in appearance and content). Photographs of Pamela are everywhere: even if only in London (the Greys have moved to Mulberry House, in Smith Square, Westminster: here Stephen has his own shining, mirrored room) or as far afield as Fallodon, Pamela cannot bear the thought that she might be forgotten; worse, that she might not rule her youngest son's heart, as she had Bim's. Stephen stares at her framed image, whether he's at the piano (white) or stretched out on the polar-bear skin with Baby Jungman, or crossing a sea of soft carpet to greet Rosamund Lehmann at the pale oak door of Wilsford. And he knows he follows her, even as he tries to break away. Everything for Stephen must be white – as it had been for Pamela – but his white, unlike hers, is Syrie Maugham white: a white that suggests no deeper meaning within, no spirituality, purity or love. Stephen's white, reflected in the perfect face with its high cheekbones, magenta lips and great mascaraed eyes, is, like his art and his protestations of affection, only skin deep.

'Will that do, Master Stephen?' (To tell the truth, Stephen has quite forgotten Louis Ford standing outside the stone parlour, arms aching with grasping the tripod, head still buried under the black cloth that Nanny Trusler is for ever trying to whisk away to the wash.)

'Oh Louis, I *am* so sorry!' – Stephen has charm, certainly, and energy: he leaps to his feet and the little card table that bears his Indian inks trembles violently. Nanny is there, to straighten it: she gazes down with pursed lips at the exotic drawings on the fine, thick paper Mr Stephen gets sent all the way from a paper mill in Somerset. 'You see, Nanny, all the little Paget girls will look delightful in these medieval dresses,' cries Stephen. He loves to explain to servants all the most esoteric secrets of his art.

'They're not all Paget girls,' Nanny says stoutly, as Louis, coming out from under the cloth at last, appears in the doorway of the stone parlour, ruffled as one of Mr Stephen's parrots down in the aviary. 'There's Lady Jane Thynne.'

A telephone – white, mounted in gold – tinkles in the living-room hall, where the polar-bear skins and deep white sofas obliterate the solemn corner chosen by Edward Grey all those years ago to sit and wait for Pamela, on the day the Foreign Secretary found himself revealing news of impending war to the Prime Minister's wife. Now Stephen, seeing Nanny Trusler still suspiciously bending over the 'stained-glass effect' he is planning for his brother's wedding at Wells Cathedral, runs with his curious leaping, bounding stride from the stone parlour into the main part of the house. Perhaps it is Virginia Woolf who rings. (In her diary she says that Stephen walked like Swinburne, an observation first made by Thomas Hardy; but he has been catty about her, in turn: 'I know what form her madness takes!' giggled at parties – at least they're all famous, which is what counts.)

'Hello – yes?'

Stephen's face falls as a 'bore' speaks on the other end. Why hadn't Louis answered? What's wrong with the man?

'I'm busy – I can't talk now,' Stephen breathes in sudden exhaustion. He decides to take a nap, in the great white lace-spread bed upstairs. Here Pamela is banished: she may rule Kit's life, by choosing the daughter of an admirer (another Pamela) as his bride; but his mother shan't encroach here, in this room where Stephen may worship none other than himself.

The bed, with its flounces and embroidered pillows freshly starched and ironed by Nanny Trusler, accepts Stephen into its embrace. Before drifting off to sleep, he thinks of his mother's emeralds – she has so little jewellery: why on earth did not dull Eddy give her more? Stephen would quite like the art nouveau bracelet, misty emeralds entwined with diamonds; it looks almost like a message from that long-gone world where Pamela still abides, and he could make it smart to wear sentimental trifles like this. Or the big emerald ring – but then Stephen remembers that the green stone was given by Pamela to her god-daughter Pamela, Christopher's future bride. And the silly girl had been foolish enough to lose the valuable heirloom almost at once (Stephen cannot think even of a pebble without endowing it with a lineage, with royal ancestry). Feeding the ducks at the Serpentine! – that's what Christopher had to tell his mother, and very embarrassed he was about it, too. All hell broke out of course – and Stephen cannot help smiling, as his blue lids close and a very faint snore comes from between the rosy lips. The young Pamela may be a clever girl, a Cambridge graduate (how tired the eye-shadowed autodidact has grown of hearing of his brother's fiancée's achievements). But she's incapable of keeping a ring

Nanny Trusler's death, to have been a fabrication, Christopher the second son, now the eldest and successor to his father's new title and fake antique castle, is compliant with his mother's demands. He has joined the family business: Margot has already seen in him a kindness in which, despite appearances and her reputation, she is not herself altogether lacking. But then Margot has annoyed Pamela once again, on the subject of Stephen's callous, flirtatious behaviour, by remarking that Pamela's family 'has no heart'.

Pamela does not think of these things as she is carried to a country where summer lingers still – and for that she is grateful: Fallodon, though near the sea, has some of the stark coldness of Glen, and Pamela – for all that Christopher, busy covering up the plasterwork ceilings in his inherited 'seat', invites her there often – has no fond memories of the place. Margot ... it was always Margot's, the ludicrous, tin-men-on-turrets 'château', which Eddy brought her to see, after he had successfully proposed in Florence and the tap of Sir Charles's fortune had been turned on. What could Margot ever have seen in the place: in the brown hills like low-brimmed hats pulled right down to the farm buildings, heather encroaching even there, as if a giant's hair had escaped and fallen halfway down his back, to become entangled with the midget race dwelling beneath him in the rain? How Pamela hates the rain! Why did Margot like to ride all day along the side of the larch wood, up the burn wood from the loch named after her brother Eddy – on to the Black Douglas land, where it is so wild she might never get home? Pamela puts it down, as she always has, to Margot's desire to show off: who else would have ridden right into her father's house on a black stallion? And who, when it's years now since she was married to the Prime Minister, would have behaved in so forward a manner when taking poor Christopher to a reception at Buckingham Palace, only a month or so ago? Kit had told his mother: he'd laughed; though he's good-looking he's shy, and Margot had grabbed his wrist, he said, just as the queue of people at Court began to move forward in procession to be presented to the King and Queen. 'Now!' Margot had hissed, pulling him – shamingly – right up to the front of the queue. Pamela's face creases in a patronising smile as she thinks of the incident, and the train, letting out a thick plume of grey smoke, races down to golden fields, beech woods and rivers that no longer have the need to race and whirl downhill.

Pamela will go on to Wilsford after the wedding and so has brought with her – it goes wherever she goes – the flowery packet in which she keeps letters and mementoes, expressions of love and psychic discoveries; and, most of all, those proofs of her dedication to children – to her children, to any children – which support her now in her continuing, terrible grief.

Here is the rose, handed to a fellow soldier by Bim near Laventie just a few days before his death at the Somme. The rose is almost black, as Pamela's hands, trembling as she opens the envelope on the endless journey south, pull it from the stiff, apologetic letter in which it is enclosed. Here – and, now that nine years have passed, it's strangely the case that Pamela suffers more anguish at the slight mishap of an aching tooth than at Bim's death itself – are his last, brave words to her:

'I forgot to tell you that I was developing an abscess in a back molar on the morning of the day we went into action. So I forthwith mounted a prehistoric bicycle, rode eight miles in sweltering heat, had gas and tooth out in a brace of shakes, and rode back, getting one or two lifts in lorries . . .'

Pamela does not trust herself to reread Bim's final letters in the train. But she knows Edward Grey's sympathies are with her: he is as steeped in the miasma of death that hangs still over the country as she herself is.

Though he has no sons of his own, Grey has lavished love on Pamela's since the death of their father; and on occasion, when the reality of youth becomes too tiresome to deal with, he retreats into thinking and writing of the fantasy children with which the era abounds. A facetious correspondence between Lord Grey of Fallodon, as he became in 1916, and his beloved Pamela shows an altercation over the authorship of *The Young Visiters*. How can Grey ever speak to Pamela again, when she insists that the true author of the disingenuous masterpiece must really be J. M. Barrie in disguise? Cannot the mother of so many artistic children (Bim's poems, David's obvious talents at mathematics and science, Stephen's extraordinary precocity) see that Daisy

Ashford is indeed no other than the writer of this entrancing book? But Pamela – who loves to pull from her floral packet the letter from Barrie to her Bim, written in a child's voice and expressing delight in her son's enjoyment of *Peter Pan* – resists him strenuously. The correspondence almost develops into a full-blown row.

They may seek innocence, this couple who have witnessed and undergone the ordeal of the carnage and its residue, the shell-shocked, stuttering survivors of the war, but for all their espousal of a very English lack of artifice, Pamela is unable to resist her native jealousy; and in this she is both childish herself and vengeful as only a grown woman can be. A few years back, when Grey, in Washington as Ambassador, had occasion to meet and be charmed by another young writer, Opal Whiteley, Pamela had fallen, in Mulberry House, into a sulk from which even the self-adulatory success of Stephen had been incapable of rousing her. Opal – who claimed, in her humble American origins, to be in receipt of a voice from her French royal past, and who went on to publish that voice to huge acclaim, not least the worshipful admiration of Lord Grey – was a little too close to Pamela for her own comfort. For isn't Pamela, with her own claims to descent from a long line of French kings – this allied with the 'child-like' simplicity for which she receives such praise – made to seem almost foolish by the writerly fame combined with modest disclaimers exhibited by Opal Whiteley? The young genius's visit to London, and to the 'great lady' of whom Grey had spoken so fondly, had not been easy.

The train winds its way through the industrial

Midlands. Pamela looks away: her meadows, briar hedges and fine lakes are quite ruined in this unnecessary part of a country she thinks of as hers. She has written in poems and prose so often of its beauties and healing powers that each scar, mill or smoke stack can only serve as reminder of the un-happiness of her marriage with the scion of an industrial family. There is not, despite the apparent 'selflessness' of Pamela Grey, much difference be-tween her and her youngest son when it comes to seeing the world in a glass of their own fashioning.

Grey, less disturbed by the satanic aspect from the window of their first-class compartment, thinks instead with satisfaction of the marriage of young Christopher to the charming Pamela. He knows his own Pamela was made anxious by the girl's apparent wild flinging of her future mother-in-law's precious emerald ring into the waters of the Serpentine. (Pamela's jewels, like her children, will always be seen to be hers.) But Grey, soother of troubled souls, diplomat, also knows the incident will soon be forgotten – after all, Pamela the mother, in picking this Pamela for her son, did, as so often before, achieve her most heartfelt desire.

Clare drives at breakneck speed – so David likes to describe his sister's recklessness at the wheel – and as he says the word 'breakneck' he rolls his eyes and his dark, handsome face seems itself to break up, as he takes one last gulp of the White Lady or the

Screwdriver that opens his day at his new club.

By now Clare knows David will have overtaken her: hangover or no, he will appear on the steps of Wells Cathedral just in time to act the usher, white carnation in buttonhole, respectful smiles and bows to Mr Asquith and Margot's daughter Elizabeth, now Princess Elizabeth Bibesco. David knows how to please; though, like the rest of the family, his real interest lies in pleasing himself. After the service – Christopher's bride is pretty enough to have merited a lunge from her about-to-be brother-in-law – he will take the bridesmaids to the reception (he'll say he's sorry they're too young for him) and then he'll shoot back to London in the Hispano Suiza, to the glittering lights he has to create himself to stave off the boredom from which he suffers so fatally. The lights are fixed in the ceiling of the new club, the Gargoyle: stars that twinkle down on the smart, the war veterans still in their twenties, the Bohemian (the press makes much of this; Stephen is envious: he plans a Grand Success gala for later in the autumn, in the dark, exciting little room where all London goes).

David has Matisses a-plenty: hung in the club, a swathe of colour seen as the first visitors of the evening step from the rickety little lift, they seem to advertise their owner's careless good taste. They are new, like the music, the cocktails – and some, at least, of the faces. The great planes of shape and colour form the background to brawls and fights when the boredom becomes inescapable. Guests, too drunk to make their way home in the dawn, sleep beneath the mountains of blue and red, the pigments of Matisse, and frown when they wake under tawdry stars that –

yet again – everyone has forgotten to turn off. There is neither night nor day at the Gargoyle; and as there is no sense of recorded time, it is always the hour to have a drink. David, as Clare knows, will not be able to wait to return to this heaven he has made; she also knows, though she is tired of making the poor joke, that David prefers the White Lady to the Manhattan because he feels, with each cruelly powerful sip, that he is putting his mother – *The White Wallet* (Pamela's book), white dresses and flowers and all – *down*. How David and Clare both struggle to free themselves from Pamela! And today, when they must kiss her in the porch of Wells Cathedral and sit piously behind her as the sober, sensible Christopher is pledged to Pamela's god-daughter, how they will pine for London! – for those bright lights again, the shops and the bars, for the romances in Rosa Lewis's Cavendish Hotel, which die as fast as a gardenia.

Clare's car, accelerating around a corner in the last lap of the journey to Somerset, runs into a high bank and sticks there, back wheels whirling. Not for the first time, she regrets having decided to drive rather than take the special train laid on for guests – but the Hawk-Ellis is the last remaining symbol of the large lump sum Eddy left her four years ago. A 'wolfish' car, as Lionel, who has by now run through all her money (they are divorced), says with pride. Why the bloody hell shouldn't she take the Hawk-Ellis? – Clare doesn't particularly want to swear, but every- one does nowadays and a car bought by one's ex- husband with one's own money is as good an opportunity to do so as any. This new development – stuck in a hedge with any chance of being on time for fan-shaped draperies of gold tissue') not lend poor Pamela the air of a lamé-clad mermaid? As for the orange, turquoise and jade for the bridesmaids – in a further dive of confidence, Stephen has to resort to stroking the familiars he has brought with him, despite Nanny Trusler's reproofs: a toad and a snake.

There are now only five minutes to go. The groom has slipped into the cathedral by a side entrance. Clare – rescued as she had imagined she would be, by a rustic character whose wife later complained at length about the amount of make-up the young lady wore, the bright dab on the cheeks, the white skin; and wondered only that the 'fast' driver of the Hawk-Ellis hadn't been shingled: she'd be just the type – Clare roars up, to the delight and consternation of those still hanging about outside. Lady Grey has already gone in, of course: that was her son David who was heard to address her as 'Darling Muth' and escort her and Lord Grey of Fallodon to their pew. It's worth standing here a moment more, though: Mr Asquith (the Earl of Oxford, but where is his notorious Margot?) is right in view, at the side of the porch, and that's his daughter and her husband, Prince Antoine Bibesco – he's funny-looking, no doubt about that. Clare, with a wicked glance at her brother David, has gone in.

Here, as in the films of that time, with their impeccable scrolls – *A Few Days Later* or *Several Years Later* – we leave the family at the wedding and

PART TWO

A TWISTED BRANCH

The memory throws up high and dry
A crowd of twisted things;
A twisted branch upon the beach
Eaten smooth, and polished
As if the world gave up
The secret of its skeleton,
Stiff and white.

T. S. Eliot,
'Rhapsody on a Windy Night',
1917

FIVE

Glen

Emma Tennant in 1942, aged four,
and her great-grandmother Emma

It's March 1941 and I'm three-and-a-half years old. On the hills at Glen, thin snow lies on heather that no-one walks over to shoot now. There's a war on, and even the garden gates have been commandeered, 'for the soldiers', Louisa tries to tell me, when I run through the unaccustomed gap on to grass shorn and grey from the frost. And 'Wait – come back – come indoors' comes another voice, so faint yet unmistakable in memory that I am bombarded by images of my earliest years: fire in the nursery chimney at Glen and the firemen as they dash into the room, holding pails; Mrs McKay in the huge basement kitchen, tossing pancakes, then handing me the pan, hand firmly over mine as the brown, spotted halo soars into the air and hangs above poor Bella's head at the sink, before falling obediently to earth; the oldest part of the house, the two rooms next to the kitchen, where we slept some of the time for fear of bombs. I see, as I hear the voice calling me in, away from the freedom of the open field, a grey head, a row of knitting, and a dark blue box of 100 Player's, with a naval face painted on the lid. And I sense the anxiety of the woman, already old, who is in sole charge of me during the war while my parents are in London, or crossing Europe to enable my father to take up his post in Turkey, by the Bosphorus Sea.

May Toomey came from a prosperous family who had been indigo growers in India, and then had lost all their money when chemical dyes (not so distant from the bleach invented at the start of the nineteenth century by Sir Charles's grandfather in Glasgow) replaced natural ones. She had come to London in search of work, at the time of the First World War, and had been taken on as nanny to my mother; now, a quarter of a century later, she was to find herself appointed my guardian and nurse in a freezing, mock-Gothic castle in Scotland where the home-made electricity failed every evening and Louisa, the only other inhabitant of this unlikely sanctuary from war, trundled home to the kennels and an ancient father at night, her strange niece Bella tagging along behind her. May must have wondered if this war would ever end, and with it the enslavement of cold, of a child's complaint of chilblains and demands for rationed chocolate; and at night, the dreams I was later told I suffered: Mother and Father rising water-logged, seaweed-crowned, in my sleep, just when May knew them to be attempting a journey home by ship and at risk from torpedoes.

There was no-one in this great, empty house for May to confide in – other than Mrs McKay, who came in to cook the dried egg and breadcrumbed rab-bit which made up our daily fare. But Mrs McKay was too cheerful – and too busy – to stop and talk. May must have been lonely (she read her way through Sir Walter Scott, so she told us, in Eddy's fine library downstairs from our nursery); and she must have tried to speak to Louisa – but there was some-thing quiet and sad about Louisa, though it took me many years, many questions May would occasionally answer, and many visits to the Walnut Room cup-board down the hall to begin to discover the reasons for Louisa's muted sadness. And it took longer still to draw up an outline of the intoxicating new region I found there, the story of my family and its past.

On this bright, cold spring day in 1941 I am too young, of course, for this to have begun to suggest itself to me. I know May only as a presence, more often benign than irritable, and the few times I've seen her upset or agitated (the chimney fire was one: as I stood by the fender, enraptured by the lava flow as it gushed on to the hearth, she seized me and later wept) I forgot with the shutter click of a child's memory. I know nothing of the history of the house, or of my family; the families I do have tend to live – in my imagination – in holes in the trees in the garden: a monkey here, a nest of squirrels there. I am aware of myself only as a tracer of paths – the bright-green carpeted path up the main stairs from the hall, past the drawings of handsome men with moustaches and oils of bonneted women and their bearded protectors; secret paths down back stairs where Louisa goes with brush and faulty Hoover; hidden ways up the wooden spiral, past the carved bird on a post so much taller than I. With my eyes closed I can find the mown path in the garden that leads up to the now gateless fence and the mauve and green hill beyond. In an instant, pursuing the call of blackbird and thrush, running up past the children's garden with its drained stone pool, I can elude my captors and plunge into the tunnel under the village road. Here, as I emerge in mud-brown light, I see the first violet, and rush to find the blue and red wild flower May calls thunder and lightning, shaking her head when asked to explain why. I know my way, at Glen;

and I am determined to get my way, too: the only time Louisa laughs is when I shout that I must be left alone, or beg her for the tenth time that day to take me down to the kennels where the shooting-dogs, pale Labradors and collies, pace their cement yards.

What becomes clear today, however, as I dash from May's fingers fumbling with my shoelaces and buttons and descend by the banister, the speediest path of all, to the main hall, is that I don't have any more idea of who I am than I do of my family or its past. I am a clean slate: I will believe anything; and my precocious knowledge of the ins and outs of Glen are no indication that I'm old for my years.

The main hall at Glen, painted white by my mother and covered in the grassy-green carpet intended to banish any remaining suggestion of a fake baronial, old-panelled-wood-and-dark-floor setting, leads in turn to a small front hall, narrow and uncheerable by reason of the pictures of dead animals that hang there. Stags with their bellies ripped open; pheasants with eyes ruby-red with blood as it wells from their dying gaze; foxes in the last throes of agony are displayed on the walls, along with the improbable picture of a young woman on a black horse mounting the front steps at Glen and preparing to ride inside (only much later did I know this was Margot: I admired her temerity and knew that Louisa, who chuckled sometimes when I pointed the picture out to her, did too).

In the hall, by a painting of dead trout often morbidly examined by me, stands a tall, thin woman. I see a frizz of hair, yellowish; a bandanna; I see a smiling face; I know I am in the presence of a stranger, but nothing more. I don't run to the door, for a change. The circular sweep of gravel, with its turfed centre and the lure of the stables beyond, where empty stalls filled with debris from past years are ripe for climbing, tussling with children from the farm, do not tempt me. Perhaps I know – for the first time in my life – that it's more polite to wait until I'm spoken to, before running off. May certainly hasn't taught me manners: the stranger must have brought them with her, in her urgent need to be heard.

'Darling,' the stranger says; but she doesn't bend to take me in her arms. I stare up past her, at the sad, dark green, Regency-stripe wallpaper, and in a corner of a picture at the splayed legs of a hind as it falls victim to a pack of hounds. 'You can call me Mummy,' the stranger says.

As I stand and stare, the door into the front hall opens and someone (Louisa? her brother Doug, the keeper, going between pantry and hall with a fish pulled out of the burn? I cannot remember which) comes down the steps and picks me up to carry me back to the nursery. My path, instead of taking me triumphantly to the turret door by way of a stone spiral staircase to the basement, an exciting, never-used route, is to be ignominiously retraced: like a baby I am handed to May, and like a baby I scream and spill out the story of the strange lady in the front hall. I see May's mouth, held in place by gossamer lines at the corners, parachute down and then close again, trembling. I cry more loudly, properly frightened now that my false mother will somehow reappear – and, as I try desperately to recall the face of the mother who comes to the nursery, sits on the fender and talks to May, a dreadful, icy doubt begins to seize me. If the stranger is my mother, then who am I?

We grow calm in the end, May and I, and I see her hand, splodged with brown freckles, as it reaches for the important-looking box and takes out a Player's cigarette. The wireless is switched on. With a heavy tread she goes to the turret pantry and I smirk with satisfaction: my traumatic experience will earn me a slice of white bread sprinkled with red, white and blue sugar granules, hundreds and thousands, as they are known. I ache for the sweetness; May puts on the kettle, which is in any case never far from the boil, and helps herself to three spoonfuls of sugar. To the soothing sound of a lady announcer's voice, we go separately into a zone of recovery.

It is impossible to say whether I saw Pamela, my father's first wife, again during the time she spent at Glen – a time offered by him, as it transpired, to allow her to get away from London and the fear of bombs. I don't know if I saw her one morning in the dining-room, walking with a vaguely agitated air around the table at the end of the room where daffodils, plentiful at that time of year, stood by the window giving on to the valley and the rain. I believe she may have been there: something about a bright, bird-like movement as I ran in alerted me to the fact she wasn't supposed to be there. But where were her two sons, my half-brothers, at this point? I have no idea.

Pamela – when I reached the stage, some years later, of learning how to open the concealed cupboard in the Walnut Room, and the photographs and books and letters fell out on to the floor – Pamela the Second was harder to imagine than my father's mother Pamela. There was no trace of her, other than a photograph torn from a magazine of Mr Asquith standing by the vaulted entrance to Wells Cathedral, with a caption stating that he attended the 'wedding of Lord Glenconner to Miss Pamela Paget'. How often did I gaze at the closed façade of the cathedral and pray for it to open, like a children's book where a dull and empty scene is transformed, at the lifting of a flap, into a circus in full swing? I had to dream the activities behind the moulded, impressive façade: my father, tall and handsome, waiting at the altar for the bride his mother has chosen for him. The slow procession up the aisle on the arm of her father . . . But maybe because I imagine a white bridal veil, which hides her pretty face and cropped '20s hair, I cannot put together this woman with the sad, ingratiating woman who wanted me as a daughter in the front hall.

My other memory of those years – when I was about five years old and my father and mother were away from Glen a great deal, so that my life revolved around the worried voice of May, the jollity of Mrs McKay and the aloofness of Louisa – also concerned a stranger, though a very different kind of stranger from Pamela's Pamela.

Bella, whom I never saw as 'lacking' – a word used to describe her by May, and only to my mother when she paid one of her visits to the nursery – was to be my companion on the new adventure, which greed and a longing for escape impelled me to embark on. That she was not a perfect cicerone for a five-year-old child in wartime, when even the quiet braes and lanes contained prisoners of war and there was always the possibility of a bomb falling out of the sky, simply never occurred to me. Bella, daughter of Louisa's brother Doug, keeper at the kennels, belonged to Glen as I did. But I must have known, too, that only Bella would go along with my forbidden journey in search of the world beyond the valley, where we were shut up for the duration of the war. She was indeed perfect, for my purposes at least: for Bella 'lacked' not only a sense of direction but also a sense of right and wrong.

I don't think my father ever saw Bella. She was small, so small that her eyes and surprisingly large, beaky nose came only just over the top of the kitchen table. Her chin – and a very slack mouth that muttered and dribbled in a kind of singsong language I could sometimes understand – was lost to view, below the rim of the thick, much-scoured, gargantuan table. Her hands, snapping at spinach, rolling a wooden pin in dough, fluttered about the sides of her head as she worked, like dancing ears.

Strong footsteps in the passage could mean my father. He might have a rabbit in his hand, and pass it in to Mrs McKay through a half-window in the passage. It was like my Pollocks Toy Theatre – Mrs McKay might be whirling and skipping from the dresser to the iron pots on the old Aga, Doug the keeper might be back from the woods with birds' tail feathers as bright as an actress's plumed hat. Bella at those times was at the sink, invisible in the gloom of the far side of the old kitchen. Her head peered into the sink and her hands were high, shedding a rapid succession of soft fingernails, the oblong and glistening potato peelings that would then go out the back for the pig. Or she was in the scullery, climbing on a chair to cut down a wood pigeon and, very occasionally, a pheasant. In the scullery, with its trough-sized stone sinks and dim light from a window that gave out on the cinder heap at the back, Bella looked particularly small. If my father came in, he would be bound to miss her in the uncertain light. But I didn't think of her as being small then, of course; for Bella was the same height as me.

One day three things happened at the same time. The first was that summer came at last to our northern valley. We'd been so long in snow, and beneath skies as grey as the heron that kept flapping down by the side of the frozen burn, that it was hard to remember the green on the trees in the wood. We stood staring at it, Mrs McKay and Bella and I. What a lovely sight it was! And I immediately found I couldn't remember at all what the winter had been like. I said I wanted to go up to the Fairy Ring. For I'd had the fairy stories of James Hogg, the 'Ettrick Shepherd', read to me and he'd written of this wood, where people could be turned to three-legged stools if they went into the Fairy Ring. I wanted to go there, though already I felt anxious that this might happen to me.

Mrs McKay said we couldn't go. Fallen trees across the path made it dangerous. And yet I knew she'd been up there with Doug's wife Kitty and their daughter; they'd been picking bilberries on the heathery hillside above the wood and their mouths and cheeks were as purple as if they'd been drinking wine up there, waiting for the fairies and witches that the Ettrick Shepherd had seen.

The next thing that happened – after the astonishing refusal of Mrs McKay to lie in the beautiful mossy circle with the new summer sun coming in through the birch leaves – was that my father (it was one of the rare times he was at Glen) came out on to the grass from another door and stood beside us. Bella, as always, had slipped into invisibility behind a wall where once, before the war and the disappearance of gardeners, there had been a peony garden. She knelt on an overgrown path, pulling at dandelion leaves. My father and Mrs McKay and I stood staring right in front of us, as if we were hoping for something to appear on the hillside opposite, out of the Ettrick wood.

My father said he was going away to the war. He would be in a very hot place, where sometimes it was over a hundred in the shade. I saw a tent, and men like Ali Baba coming in and standing with my father. He said the dried figs we ate sometimes had probably come from there.

So my father and mother must already have left in the old Wolseley for the war when I formed a plan to leave Glen myself – and this was the third thing that happened that day.

May kept a small purse for me, in which pocket-money was stored. I found it easily, in the drawer that smelt of biscuits, in the table by her bed in the night-nursery. I ran down to the old kitchen, which was empty except for birds hanging from the ceiling – and Bella. I told her we were going away.

Bella put down the half-plucked bird on the great stone ledge by the sink. She had a bootlace in her pocket and she tied it round her hair. We went out the back, and then climbed a flight of steps to join the front drive at a point where we couldn't be seen. The drive was overgrown at the sides with bright green moss, like the moss in the Fairy Ring. Bella tried to kneel down and pull out the moss, but it would have taken too long to tidy up a mile of road, and I tugged at her arm. I wanted to walk to Innerleithen, our nearest small town, and buy an ice cream – then climb up to the wood and walk along paths drying out their last year's mulch, to the Fairy Ring. I didn't want to be turned into a piece of wood, but I thought that day that I was bound to see a fox, or a kingfisher perhaps, flashing over the trees.

Nothing seemed to go right. The road was very hot, and I saw that we really had forgotten about summer, because my feet in their Clarks sandals itched with a sort of dry heat that made me almost decide to go back. But I wanted the ice cream, which would be served at St Ronan's Café by Mr Gigli or his wife. St Ronan was the patron saint of this small, grey Scottish town. Mr and Mrs Gigli, perhaps because they were Italian, were thought to short-change people. But they poured reckless quantities of raspberry syrup on the ice cream and you could carry it over the patch of fusty lino to a table. It was thinking of this that kept me going – even when Bella began to lag behind.

We were just on the last stretch of road, the

straight stretch between the old manse and Traquair village, where James Hogg said witches still lived in his own time, when I stopped and looked back and saw how far away Bella was. She was certainly small now, standing on the road with the stern face of the old quarries to one side of her, overgrown with heather, and the forest, thick and white-barked with mottled patches on the trunks, looming on the other. She was as small as a three-legged stool. I felt as frightened as if we were already in the wood. But I walked on, and soon I crossed the Tweed and was in the outskirts of the small town. I looked round once and Bella was completely out of sight. But before I'd got that far I'd seen a group of men coming along the road. They looked as if they'd been pulled through a hedge backwards, these men, and some of them carried picks or spades. I ran faster, past Traquair, the old white house on the edge of the Tweed, and then past the Traquair Arms. Before long I was in the lonely main street where St Ronan's Café stood.

Mr Gigli was talking about the men in the road when I came in. He wanted to show he had nothing to do with them, although, like him, they weren't English. 'The enemy,' Mr Gigli said. He was short and fat, and his hair was black and shiny with brilliantine. 'B-risoners of Wuh.'

I didn't know what Mr Gigli meant. He was directing his remarks to a man who looked like a shepherd, who had come in for a bottle of St Ronan's ginger beer. The shepherd was dour and silent, so Mr Gigli had to talk to me. He pushed down a scoop of vanilla ice cream, which was really made of whale fat, or so we were always being told by Mrs McKay.

'Bloody Germans,' Mr Gigli said. 'Why they no just shoot them, I say?'

In his excitement Mr Gigli added another scoop to the existing one in the ribbed glass dish. I kept as quiet as the shepherd, hoping Mr Gigli wouldn't see his mistake. The bottle of raspberry syrup came off the shelf and there was the usual rush of sticky red juice on the ice cream, but this time, of course, with more of it to cover. I gave Mr Gigli half a crown from my purse and went to the table and sat down.

Bella never turned up in the café. But the shepherd had recognised me; he went out and waved down a man in a car who worked on the Glen farm and I was told quite severely that I would be given a lift home. I had to finish the ice cream in a rush. When I went out in the street and got into the unfamiliar car, the man said he'd seen Bella on the road and we'd stop and pick her up on the way back. He seemed very angry: petrol rationing made this unnecessary trip another headache for anyone working on a farm as remote as Glen. And when we found Bella, who'd hardly moved at all since I last looked back and saw her so small, she climbed into the car like a dog. She was giggling a bit, and dribbling too from her big, slack lips. I held her hand, because it was dancing so fast on my knee. 'POWs,' the farming man said.

May and Mrs McKay were no kinder when we were dropped at the back door and went in. First, Mrs McKay slapped Bella. She said Bella was old enough to know better. Then May said I had no right to take the purse without asking her. She demanded it back. And when she forced me to say how much I had paid for the ice cream and she looked inside the purse, she said Mr Gigli had short-changed me. Neither she nor Mrs McKay was in any mood to hear that Mr Gigli had given me a double portion of ice cream, in his agitation over the prisoners of war.

'Germans,' Mrs McKay said. I was made to go to bed early. I was lonely in the room in the basement, with the sound of Mrs McKay bustling in the kitchen and the wireless going on and off.

'What would I say to your father and mother?' May came and said at the door, before turning off the light. A tormenting streak of the brightness of a northern summer evening still showed under the door when she had gone.

My father had been sent to be head of SOE in Cairo. The SOE organised resistance in the war, and this was the summer of 1943. He had agreed to receive a delegation of Greek guerrillas, from a landing-strip in the mountains of Thessaly, at his headquarters in Cairo. These resistance fighters made up what was known as 'the Andarte delegation'. Their bravery and cunning in ambushing the Germans who occupied their villages was well known. But Winston Churchill considered them to be little better than bandits. It was my father's hope, along with that of Brigadier Myers, who brought the six guerrillas from the tiny airstrip at Nevaida, that these men would be allowed a say in the running of their country and of the military. They set off with Myers on 9th August in a small plane; the usual method, of going by caique to Turkey, was considered too risky. They arrived on 10th August. But their hopes were soon dashed. The Foreign Office was very much against the SOE in this matter.

Churchill wanted the King restored in Greece. He didn't want the 'bandits' to have anything at all.

The Germans were strung out in the stone villages of Greece. My father had told me that 'we' were at war with the Germans. As I lay in my half-sleep in the basement kitchen flat at Glen, I saw the German prisoners on the road between Traquair manse and the small town, and I saw them run round the town and shoot and shoot, as in the Pathé newsreels that May and Mrs McKay sometimes took me to see. The small town went up in a cloud of grey smoke. I woke and crawled out of bed, to look out of the tiny window in the bedroom. Up above the Ettrick forest, which was untouched by the war, a line of faint red showed, for a red-sky-at-night-shepherd's-delight sunset. Beyond the red was desert, where my father sat in his tent. He had a desk like the one in the library upstairs and his fingers drummed on a leather top the colour of dried figs. He wore a white sheet, because it was so hot.

The Greek guerrillas had to go home, in the end. The FO would still grant them nothing, because they were Communists. The FO was set on the King.

In October 1944 my father was recalled from Cairo. He, along with two others who had agreed on the necessity of helping the Greek resistance fighters, had been forced to resign. I can't remember any particular moment when he and my mother were back in the house again. The story of my running away to the small town was told, but it must have sounded quite unimportant.

With the return of my parents, I left my room in the basement and moved back upstairs, to rooms where light came in. The next time I went down to the kitchen, it was to find a hand of bananas lying on the ledge of the half-window in the passage. Mrs McKay was making a terrific fuss of them.

My father had brought back this spreading hand of pale-green fingers from Cairo. And to everyone they seemed to symbolise a world without war. Mrs McKay told me again and again that I'd never seen such a thing before in my life. But the bananas didn't ripen properly, and in the end Mrs McKay had to cook them with brown sugar and raisins found in a tin left over from before the beginning of the war.

SIX

Visitors

Glen in the 1920s

Glen was cold and bare, in those years of war and after-war, when frost made intricate lace patterns inside the windowpanes. Louisa, for ever trudging between nursery, dining-room and hall with scuttles of coal and kindling sticks, seemed to have dried and withered with the passing of time, to have been polished smooth as driftwood, worn by memories I could feel she had no intention of letting go.

The house itself manifested the same combination, of poverty and hidden riches. Like the ornate ceilings, dados and cornices, painted or covered over with hardboard, and the boastful turrets and flights of unnecessary steps, the past was forbidden and invisible as the secret chamber of Bluebeard's castle, the inhabitants of that now remote country having vanished, apparently for ever, from their former haunts. Traces could be found in high boxrooms and attics: a wicker saddle for a pony, suggesting the trips up to build a twig fire and make tea at the loch, of which May had spoken, in summers before the war. (The pony had strayed, everyone walked home, she said, and her voice still bore the wonder and disappointment of the day.) Albums of old photographs – of a prehistory to which no-one could provide the key: the stiff, hooped dresses, the grumpy, Queen Victoria faces, the men like cut-outs in their serried rows; it seemed to me then that men were born to stand or sit in rows: the School Photograph; the Shooting Party; the Club (in this case a rowing club,

with the words *True Blue* in fancy lettering underneath: could that really be my grandfather, as May
doubtfully pronounced?) – all these were on high,
thrown on top of one another and, in many cases,
irretrievably squashed by big, dark blue trunks bearing the name TENNYSON. Who was this? What was
inside? 'Just Harold's things,' May said, and then her
voice tailed off again. I wondered, would Harold ever
come to reclaim the trunks, in their low-ceilinged
homes? Would he climb up, past the wooden pelican at
the top of the spiral stairs, and stand looking down at
the floor where guests and my mother and father had
their rooms? Or had he gone where so many of the rest
had gone, into a place from which even their names,
with the gradual passing of the cold days and long,
dark nights, would no longer be spoken by anyone?

It was impossible to answer, and the question of
Harold – striking me each time I crawled from the
smallest boxroom, its door a mere two feet in height
and therefore easier for me than for anyone else to
reach and to hide myself in – became a paradigm for
the whole state of affairs in this house, with its false
ceilings, empty rooms and bland expanses of white
paint. I had left behind me the attic at Glen, which
could be said to be the most intriguing of them all: a
glass floor in one corner revealed, below the contours
of the nursery bathroom, the wooden lavatory – a
Victorian throne; another corner housed a swarm of
bees, sleepy or dead and with their honeycombs
scattered about them on the floorboards. My knee
was grazed, as it was each time by attempting an exit
up a short wooden ladder inside the attic, which led
to the minuscule door. And, as I climbed, my eye was

caught – as it was on every occasion when I tried to get out and thought myself stuck there, immured for ever while May smoked and knitted miles away in the day-nursery – my eye was caught, in my inevitable panic, by the dull corner of yet another of Harold's dark blue trunks.

One day – before I had discovered the cupboard in the Walnut Room, and thus was able to go in search of Louisa, of May, of anyone who might tell me stories to satisfy my new obsession with the past – I heard footsteps running down the back stairs and knew they were neither the dragging tread of Bella nor the almost silent, swift progress of Louisa through the house. I was up in the highest room at the time: for some reason that had never been clear to me, it was known as The Kennels; with its hard, lumpy bed, bright mural over the windows of the faces of beagles, terriers and stags and its general air of abandonment, it was a perfect place to examine some of the spoils the attics could provide. Dead flies on the sills meant that even Louisa, with her martyred determination to do the work of all the maids gone with war and changing fortunes, never came in here, and the boar's head over the door (which I took trouble not to glance up at when I entered) was as moth-eaten as the rest of this unvisited part of the house. But another advantage of The Kennels was that its windows looked out to the front: to the stables, and the circular sweep of gravel with its central saucer of green. Here my teacher at the Glen village school, Mrs Wright, had performed a perfect somersault in a demonstration of the art to me, the pupil from Glen House, and my mother and father had invited her in for tea. Here, now, came a black car – not the broken-down old Wolseley, which took us sometimes to the loch but couldn't get us up the steep brae on the way back, so that we all had to get out to push. Here, today, was a new and different car; and within it a beaky profile, under a strange, old-fashioned hat.

I ran down the stairs, back stairs dark and carpeted in a hard, black cord which, together with the gloom from walls of a hospital green and a skylight above clogged and musty with age, made the journey always a perilous one – and I saw, as I ran through the door into the great white expanse of the hall, that it was indeed Louisa who had descended with such excited, unfamiliar footsteps from the upper floors of the house. (She had used one of the rooms there as a look-out post – perhaps she too had wanted to see the surprising visitor.) Red-faced and shiny, Mrs McKay was at her side, and though they turned and looked at me, their usual expressions had changed. Then my father and mother came from the drawing-room at the far end of the hall; both also looked at me as if I wasn't there; and both, as I saw to my relief, smiled and talked animatedly, as if a rocket had exploded in the garden beyond the quiet room, once the billiard room, which my mother had created so that my father, in his second marriage, could start anew.

'It's too ridiculous,' my father said. But he gazed for reassurance at my mother, and she still laughed – at me, as I thought at first, for I knelt on the window seat in the hall and, looking out at the gravel sweep, could see that the black car and its occupant had disappeared from sight.

'There's no reason she *should* like it here now,' my mother said.

The event was talked about all day, both in the kitchen and at lunch, as my parents sat over plates of rabbit – today transformed by Mrs McKay into an orange-coloured stew, which, in order to gain attention, I peevishly refused to eat.

The talk was of my father's aunt Margot and her eccentric visit to Glen. She would do this sometimes – though this was the first occasion, it appeared, when she had refused to come into the house at all. Burning, even in her eighties, with a possessive love, she paid lightning visits to Château Margot, as Glen was known in the days of old Sir Charles, visits from Mr Gladstone and all. The old Bart's opulence had shown in the wealth of overdone detail, but Margot found herself a stranger in the new, constrained Glen. She had seen the drawing-rooms where once she and her beautiful sister Laura had entertained the young men who proposed marriage to each daughter in turn – and seen them relegated to the dustsheets of war and oblivion.

This time Margot had had herself driven straight up to the loch – so I heard said, as I sat scowling over my untasted meal. And I saw – for already the country of my great-aunt and my grandmother's past was bursting from its shell, flying in my imagination to take root in the few locales I knew to fit it – I saw Margot on the bench by the loch, looking out over black water so clear that the stones and weeds seemed magnified, on a day when the ripples brought by a north wind didn't cloud the picture there. Margot went into the boathouse, curtsied to the King and Queen enthroned there with their Court, and, seizing my father's wrist, pulled him across the floor to bow to King George and Queen Mary. (For, as my father remembered this episode from his youth, so it was acted out before my eyes. My mother laughed even more, then: 'I like Margot,' she said; and the subject, like everything else in the closed house, had gone.)

Only one other scene, related with an equal enjoyment in the dining-room that day, came to tease my mind's eye – and this was the news that Margot, despite the war, went dancing on frequent occasions with Stephen at the Savoy. But, however hard I tried to transform the old racquet court halfway down the back road into 'The Savoy', and to envisage the whirling figure in the odd hat (very thin, with a nose that almost met her chin, which was all I'd seen in the black car) in the dance I'd learnt from Mrs McKay down in her sitting-room, the Hokey-Cokey, the dramatised picture never really came off. It was impossible to imagine an old woman such as Margot kicking her legs up in the air, like the girls at the Christmas dance up at the Village Hall. In any case I had no idea of the appearance or dancing ability of my father's brother, my uncle Stephen.

The secrets of sex fell on me, literally, not long after this, from the cupboard flush with the wall, the cupboard cunningly contrived to appear no more than a panel in an ugly, wearying room that no-one ever wanted to enter.

The Walnut Room, of a suspiciously brand-new-looking grained wood, lay behind the small drawing-room constructed by my mother in order, as I came to think later, to render my father's silences on the subject of his mother Pamela, and of the past in general, more understandable: if no-one other than long-gone billiard players had ever frequented this room, then the ghosts otherwise free to roam the halls and 'Old' Drawing-Rooms were less likely to come in there. Whether they felt at liberty to enter the Walnut Room I don't know – for all my mother's remarks that to be alone at Glen in the war and go up to bed at night was not a pleasant experience, I never saw or heard anything of an other-worldly nature. But their remains – the letters, Pamela's white vellum diaries, the scrolls and paraphernalia of my father's father's Lord High Commissionership of Scotland – were all stored here, in a cupboard that didn't even merit the facetious titles of the faked book spines in the drawing-room next door. (These, as was sheepishly confessed by my father, were the brain-child of Pamela. *Handel on the Art of Tuning* proclaimed the way into a cupboard as disappointing, with its stack of old bezique and piquet and mah-jong sets, as the Walnut Room was rich with buried stories of the past.)

The day I found the cupboard was the day of my never-before-seen uncle's visit to Glen. I'd noticed Louisa's pallor, her quick, shuffling rush to dust out the Valley Room, the best and largest bedroom on the first floor of the house, and I'd followed her there, to watch the painstaking lighting of the fire in the small grate (it was late summer and bitterly cold,

with rugs piled into the Wolseley for tea at the loch
and visits to the wool mill in Innerleithen a frequent
treat). The one bar of electric fire, all the 'hydro-
electric' method of lighting and heating Glen could
afford, gave off a pathetically small amount of heat
in the huge room. Louisa and I stood staring at it for
a while, but neither of us made any comment.

It was after this, as if driven down to the un-
promising Walnut Room and its hidden treasure by
the imminent arrival of one of Pamela's 'jewels', that
I made my find. I must have seen the door's knob of
wood, a wood different from walnut, on previous
visits to this room without a function, which looked
out on a lawn, a tall silver birch tree and not much
else. I walked over to the panel, pulled at the knob,
and received from the highest shelf and subsequently
from the shelves below an avalanche of the frozen
tears of my grandmother and her world.

By the time I was old enough to understand
unhappiness – not the grief of a mother who has lost
a son, but simple, daily, sexual unhappiness – I had
also begun to learn that those people in the 'past', a
past I considered definite and immutable, were themselves products of a constantly changing present: they
also had memories at which I could only begin to
guess; their prehistory was as important to them as
their own history had become crucial to me. I learnt,
too, that the sole cause of this unhappiness – which,
in my family, was to assume the proportions of Greek
tragedy – could be discovered, again and again, in the
loss, the thwarting of love. Patterns and repetitions,
as densely interwoven as the birds and leaves of
Pamela's mother's William Morris designs (every-

where at Glen: I played in my nursery under bright-eyed birds and red berries, slept in the shadow of green and yellow yew), became clear as one secret after another fell into my hands. Unhappiness – caused by a life where love, diverted, must flow underground and feed those for whom such intensity of feeling is not naturally intended: children, siblings, friends – was also, as I came to see, rooted in greed, in the need and passion for money. Not a ripple on the loch at Glen failed to reflect this pride and wastefulness. (Wasn't the loch itself, under its tall ravine, man- and therefore money-made? The black water, imprisoned against its will, circled the sluice endlessly but without escape.) Sex – which took longer to understand – was as closely bound up in this fatal pattern as its accomplice, money. My grandmother had married – or been forced by her parents to marry – for money. The marriage she had arranged for my father, in order for her own possessive love of her children to continue unhindered, contained no love and produced only further unhappiness. In each case, as half-stories gleaned from May or Louisa, dusty letters in floral packets and anguished pencilled reports of signals from another sphere informed me, the loss of one person – or sometimes, as I thought with Margot, of a place, Glen (though I was wrong here) – was the underlying reason for a lifetime's unhappiness. I certainly became convinced this was true of Pamela.

But on the day of my first harvest of the past in the Walnut Room, I thought none of this, of course – besides, Pamela's most intriguing 'jewel' was at that minute just arriving at the front of the house. Caught

My uncle's visit turned out to be a disappointment. He stayed only one night in the room called the Valley, because of its view of the portion of Ettrick forest that runs along the valley side: perhaps, haunted by the creatures that the Scottish Gothic imagination had planted there, he was simply frightened and decided to leave. It came to me later – though I couldn't formulate why – that something else at Glen frightened poor Stephen. It had to do with the word love. I don't think, for my mother was naturally reserved and May too absorbed in her daily routine to rise above it, that I'd ever heard the word used so often, and certainly not with such passionate intensity. Stephen, from the moment he was ensconced in the tall, cold room Louisa had taken such trouble to prepare for him – or rather, from the time he first released himself from the room and from the bewildered, chattering birds he had brought north as company – cried out his love of each object, every occasion, as if this love would bring him magically back to the radiant life and beauty proclaimed in his letters (frequent, multi-inked) to my father from Wilsford. 'Oh, Elizabeth (to my mother), *what* a wonderful place for a picnic! Oh I do *love* picnics – don't you, Christopher? I do so *love* being here –'

This particular occasion, the sole day (as it transpired) of Stephen's visit to Glen, was, I suppose, for all participants except me, especially hard to love. The rain fell with maddening monotony – it was cold, too: we were driven from the steep grass bank above the shore of the loch into the boathouse, and here, instead of the fire we always built outside, we were forced to try, in the tiny grate, to boil a kettle on a bunch of damp twigs. 'I *love* the hiss of a kettle as it gives off steam,' cried my uncle hopefully. He ran, pink-streaked legs now goose-bumped with the cold, out on to the grass bank, now almost invisible in the rain, and puffed as he went on, as far down the side of the black water as the wild cherry tree, which leans out over the loch, craggy and gnarled, its small, bitter fruit dropping at this time of year into ripples stung with rain. 'Oh, Elizabeth! Wouldn't it be fun to catch a trout and have *truite bleu*? I *love* eating like this and throwing my coat down to sit!'

I had my fishing rod, a short, childish thing given me by my father – who tied the worms on too, for our expeditions up the burn to the loch, rain or shine, trying for trout in the shallow pools where the wild nasturtiums grow. Using my uncle's ridiculous request as an excuse, I slipped from the boathouse and up into the copse of straggling larches behind; then down to the rough stones by the water's edge. I would catch a trout, for the first time alone – and if unsuccessful here, I would row the boat, which sat in the boathouse patient, as I imagined it, as a horse that knows its rider will come and untie the chafing knot as it rocks on rough water. I would row over to the island where a small house, legacy of Pamela's 'love' for her children, would shelter me if a storm got up. I'd sit in the boat as my father did, anchor on the deep loch bed, and I would catch a fish.

As it happened, Stephen's mood suddenly broke – or at least I suppose it did – for the next thing I knew all the picnic gear was being loaded into the Wolseley, parked like a forgotten, rusting god in the savage landscape by the side of the road to Loch

Eddy. My father sat very quiet at the wheel as we drove slowly home over the lumpy road. It was necessary for all of us to get out at the foot of the small brae. But here Stephen vanishes, as he was shortly to do from Glen itself, from memory. He may have come down to dinner that evening – I ate in the nursery and couldn't know. Certainly, next morning he had gone: Louisa, lips pursed, hoovered the bird-seed and parakeet droppings from the Valley Room floor. I felt cheated and let down – it seemed the visitors from the past would give almost nothing of themselves, with my great-aunt Margot avoiding the house and going straight up to the loch alone, and my uncle coming to the house and then up to the loch – but refusing, in the end, to stay with us a day longer.

The word love stayed in my mind: my father had said Margot loved Glen – and I knew I felt as she did, that nothing could ever take this place away from me. But only many years later did it suggest itself to me that another love, less innocent, had caused my uncle to leave his father's home. Stephen's love for Pamela – who had never loved it here, had despised Glen and wanted only Wilsford or Clouds, her parents' house – had ended any hope of his enjoying himself in a simple way with his elder brother, whom he certainly did love. Pamela's love for her children had divided and tormented them. Stephen went south (this time, and doubtless at my father's insistence, by train and not by Daimler). Doug from the kennels drove him to the station at Galashiels. And I woke that night worrying that the birds had been forgotten and left behind on the station platform, to suffer as my uncle had done, in the cold.

SEVEN

Secrets

Paula Long, *c.* 1920

I began to learn the secrets of first love – of the love of one sister for another – when I came face to face with the beautiful, long-dead Laura, sister of Eddy and Margot, whose portrait, in stained glass, had been executed by Burne-Jones and placed in the little turret off the room May and I shared – the night-nursery, as the crepuscular Morris foliage on the walls emphasised. Here, in the Barrie atmosphere that Pamela insisted on wherever she settled, it seemed possible that the lovely young woman Louisa spoke of with such reverence might step from the gold, blue and white glass of her Pre-Raphaelite likeness and look in on me. I lay awake, listening to May's comforting snores, and waited for the curtain to the turret to be pushed aside. I knew Laura, from the pictures and poems and word games in the Walnut Room cupboard. And I came to understand, from the way Louisa spoke of her (Louisa's mother had come to work at Glen much in the same capacity as Louisa did now: she had listened to bells as they summoned her from floor to floor – Clematis Room, Oak Room, Valley Room – and had run, up and down, with hip baths and scalding water, and baskets with dresses and petticoats, freshly starched and ironed) – I learnt, from the way Louisa spoke when she talked of her mother and then of Laura, who had married the handsome Alfred Lyttelton and died giving birth to their child, that no-one had escaped being in love with Laura. Margot least of all.

Louisa would talk of her mother's memories of the sisters: they were inseparable, she said; and we went together to the Old Drawing-Room where Sir Charles, small and with a white, pointed beard, looked across at his daughter Laura. He appeared, for one fleeting instant, before closing his expression of animated approval, to belong in our age with us. The sense of his feelings – benign, shrewd, proprietorial – for his two most famous (or notorious) daughters, was so strong that I would run to the front hall to see the portrait of Margot there, saucy in her black riding habit on the horse, equally black and well groomed, on which she rode straight into the house and up the stairs. But by the time I returned to catch a conniving smile or mock-disapproving frown from her sister and father, the moment had gone. A great-aunt, whose legendary charm had filled the Walnut Room cupboard with passionate mourning at the time of her early death, was returned to a Victorian picture, and a not particularly good one, at that.

The icon in stained glass in the night-nursery was more inspiring. Through it I strained to enter the world of complicity between Laura and Margot. And finally, when I was old enough, I was allowed their room, the Doocot, as my own, and sat imagining their conversations and philosophical word games with the young men invited to go up late at night and talk and laugh with them there. Sometimes, though I had no companion of my own (my younger brother, Toby, was out on the moor whatever the weather; and I was ten when my sister Catherine was born), I came to feel the love between Laura and Margot. It explained, or so I thought, Margot's eccentric visit to Glen and her refusal to enter a house changed since the days of her youth. For her, Laura still lived here, at Glen as it had been. It was hardly surprising she chose to go up to the boathouse and the black water of the loch, to think of Laura there.

What was difficult, in that time when all seemed empty, half-hidden or plastered-over, with only a young child's vague grasp of history (there was the Great War; the sound of May's wireless as it crackled with bulletins of the present one; the sad, impossibly noble face of Bim as he looked out from his pencilled drawing in the hall), was to put together Pamela and her life and loves and vitality – and vulgarity, as May hinted, wanting to compare my mother's family favourably with my father's over her knitting needles (but they were never mentioned, any more than my father spoke of his) – with Margot and her world. Did Pamela scorn Margot? (I suspected she did.) Did Margot find her sister-in-law hopelessly artsy and affected? It took another visit to the Walnut Room to tell me of this – and by then, Pamela's obsession with her own past had shown itself to be stronger than any rivalry or reconciliation within her husband's family. A packet of letters, in a floral design, made the subject of love arise more urgently still, in my quest for an understanding of her history. The letter to Pamela from the man who had broken her heart was folded between thank-you notes from H. H. Asquith and the repressed infatuation of Sir Edward Grey. Harry Cust wrote to my grandmother saying he dreamed of her 'insistently'. He wanted her back.

At roughly the same time – though my imagination, working unaided, may have supplied a secret father and a heartbroken mother in readiness for its arrival – the photograph of a dead baby slid into my keeping from the shelf of a desk in the Doocot Room and was put away by me, locked in a drawer, so no-one could ever take it from me. May, taking one look and saying it wasn't 'nice' to keep staring at the tiny head so carefully wrapped in a white shawl that was its shroud, clearly had no idea of the identity of the child. I had to depend on Louisa, whose eyebrows went together as I held the black and white print under her gaze. 'Oh, that's the baby,' she said. And, as I waited, the information came out, almost in spite of herself. 'Hester,' Louisa said. 'Now you put that back where you found it and come down to feed the dogs' – this a bribe, I saw. 'Where on earth you dig out these things I can't say.'

'Of course, everyone was in love with Pamela. But she never recovered from the first one – she had a crisis of nerves!'

The speaker, a tall woman with long strides – and wearing 'slacks', as May dubiously refers to the new post-war fashion – is walking ahead of me along a path by the side of a pine wood, about two miles from the house at Glen. I am twelve years old: my short hair is held back with a slide and at night a 'plate' re-trains my uneven teeth. No-one has thought to confide in me like this before, and the few questions I ask of this surprising guest are, I know, more ill-formed and childish than they need to be. We are on the 'Saturday walk' – thus named, as far as I know, because it goes further than most of the other Glen expeditions, leading the walker right down the back road almost to the kennels, then rising up by the side of the dark wood and straight out on to heather, offering a scrambling return along the side of the mountain over falling shale and twisted roots that turn the foot.

None of this matters as long as I can be with Paula – for that is her name, and, as I must have sensed then, the slightly masculine ring to it, along with the never-before-seen-on-a-female trousers, give her a glamorous, androgynous air.

Paula is beautiful. My mother says this many times a day, while my father looks off into the distance, apparently totally lacking any interest in the woman, middle-aged now, who had been a friend – perhaps more – in his youth. Paula, photographed by Cecil Beaton in her heyday, had been a Flapper, a Bright Young Thing. She is of my father's generation rather than my mother's: to me, she holds the secrets of the past before war's blankness, scarcity and sheer monotony erased the fun, and the memories too. Better still, Paula seems to want to confide in me – I, whose visits to the Walnut Room and the attics have left me with little other than a vague sense of the people who once lived here, a recognition more of the sensations I experience when I look into the photographs or, for the thousandth time, pore over Bim's account of the trenches or Harry Cust's love letter from the floral packet labelled, in Pamela's elegant hand, 'Letters From Notable Writers', than any real idea of the feelings of the dead. I know Paula *knows* – above all, I begin to suspect she is as keen to talk as I am, about the destructive, fatally fascinating subject of love.

'And Harry Cust – well, they all said he had the most perfect fingernails, you know.' Paula laughs, and stops by the edge of the wood for me to catch up. We see ahead of us a green, hidden valley, one of my favourite spots at Glen, with a remote shepherd's cottage at the crest and behind, rising above the customary shelter of Scots firs and pines, the huge purple hillside. 'He was before my time, really – but one heard, of course – he simply had to be in love every minute of the day!' Paula laughs again, the cigarettes she smokes in such profusion audible in her husky voice. I stand with her by the curve of the land, and thrill at the audacity of the woman who can speak of being in love like this – a subject my mother would never mention. I look up at my new friend (she has already told my parents she likes my company so much that we shall go for a walk together whenever I want to) and I stay silent, in the hope she will go on. I'm too shy, as yet, to press for information; besides, Paula appears to wish to follow her own pattern of thoughts uninterrupted. 'I suppose your brother seems tremendously old to you,' she continues at last, when we have skirted the valley and stand by a low wall, ready to climb over and on to empty hill. 'He's twenty-two or -three, isn't he? And seems such a baby to me. But so *marvellously* good-looking – everyone must be just mad about him, wouldn't you say?'

Even the most inexperienced listener would have

understood here that Paula, with her longing inflec-
tions on the subject of handsome men – and the sly,
sidelong glances she sent me at the mention of my
elder half-brother's name – was what Mrs McKay
described, after a Christmas party up at the Village
Hall and an exhibition by Geordie the cowman's wife
Kitty of 'the jitterbug' when the party was ordained
to be reels, as 'man-mad'. Paula had clearly fallen in
love (after skipping over my father, a beau of past
years) with my father's eldest son, Colin. He was certainly good-looking. But, apart from the excellence of
his fingernails, I had not yet heard enough about
Harry Cust. Alone, I had wondered at Pamela's
receiving so blunt a request for the resumption of a
love affair, when she was already married and sur-
rounded by children. Now here was a teacher and
companion who said she remembered my grandmother well, and could tell me more of Harry Cust.

Paula climbs the wall with ease, trousered legs
putting my kilt (I am at the stage when the family
tartan, invented by a cousin in the Highlands shortly
before the Great War, is not yet an embarrassment)
for the first time in its proper perspective. She lets out
one of her low film-star laughs at the way the green
and mauve garment snags on the stones. 'It looks all
right on someone of your age,' she reassures me as we
walk on, 'but really and truly, I don't think Clare
should wear a kilt, do you, darling? The knees, and
those terribly white legs – people used to say your
aunt bathed in asses' milk, you know, for her skin.
And her face is very smooth, of course – but those
purple lips!'

I had to give up the subject of Pamela's first love for

now – this I could recognise from the way, when my aunt Clare's name came into the conversation, a kind of lull took place, with nothing else mentionable, until the subject was exhausted and the speakers could move on.

'I wonder why she wears that net on her hair?' I dutifully venture, in order to set Paula off again.

'Oh, she thinks she looks like Vivien Leigh,' says Paula in an offhand way, and I see, for the first time, that my aunt's foibles of dress, rudeness and arrogance are not to be a main topic between us. Again, I should have guessed more cleverly: Paula wishes to return to the subject of my elder half-brother as much as I want to hear of my grandmother's long-lost love. And now, as if to trade in one obsession for another, she throws me a morsel of information, her fast pace setting her ahead of me on the narrow sheep's path along the side of the hill.

'Harry was – well – a man who loved simply every woman he met. But he loved Pamela – "my darling little Pamela" he used to call her – more than any of the others, so I always heard. He was fair, you know. I'm never sure about fair men, are you? But he wasn't rich – that was too bad, wasn't it? And Pamela had to be taken to India to recover, when poor Nina pretended to be pregnant and Harry had to marry her. Oh dear, I shouldn't be telling you this, should I? And on the way back, she saw Eddy, your grandfather, in Florence and he proposed. He was a charming man, but not like Harry Cust – Harry was so brilliant, he ran some paper, darling, and your brother reminds me of him a little bit, or what I heard of him anyway. And he was found crying in the grand Astor office –

126

Astor owned the paper and then he sacked the wretched Harry – he was crying for Pamela!'

Paula, walking so fast I have to run to keep just behind her, throws out a final comment to the effect that Eddy, not to her own taste, had been fair, too – 'Your father, always so dark, such dark looks, darling' – and we start to descend, as the path winds down above the farm buildings at Glen. I gulp with anxiety – how can I ask my question? What words can I possibly use, when what I want to know is whether Harry and Pamela did find themselves reunited, like the heroine and her love in the *Woman's Own* stories I buy from Smail's the Stationers in Innerleithen? Paula must know I need the answer. But we're down by the hayloft in the farm before I blurt out my question – and then it emerges as the wrong question after all.

'When did Harry die?' I say to the striding figure, beside me now on the rough road pitted with holes since the outbreak of war.

'Oh, in the last war, sweetie. It was too tragic. He wore himself out, you see – about a year before the end of the war, I suppose.'

I walk back down through the gate that leads from the farm into the garden at Glen, while Paula asks me her own questions: do I know who my elder half-brother is in love with right now? Is it that pretty girl Rachel, who came over to tea? There must be plenty of lovely girls – 'all mad about him, darling,' Paula says with satisfaction as we come down the last flight of steps in the garden and climb another, smaller flight to walk into the house.

* * *

Since the end of the war a season of summer visitors to Glen has established itself: August, as might be expected, with each room packed with members of the family who look warily at each other as they go up and down the stairs or into a dining-room where meals are cleared only to announce the next. The gong booms for dinner when aunts and cousins have barely finished tea; breakfast, sat over by my ponti-ficating other half-brother James, makes way for lunch, meat stews and grouse slowly replacing the rabbit dishes of the war. My father, carving the joint with a knife so long and thin it seems a miracle that food can be conjured by its blade, first mixes a salad dressing. And, inevitably, the same discussion, though no-one listens to anyone else: sugar and mustard, or plain vinegar and oil? The glass bottles with their silver hats tremble in his hand as the tedious argument goes on (my aunt Clare, probably, telling May, for lack of a better audience, that a good dressing must contain garlic and she never finds it here).

I remember, when I see the control my father exerts in order not to lose his temper with his sister (my mother has already been snubbed by her this morning – and now, as I come in muddy with Paula from the Saturday walk, the snooded head turns on the sofa, *The Times* crossword is laid aside and a 'silvery' voice announces that 'Emma looks like a Flemish page-boy!'), what Louisa had whispered to me once, on the subject of my father's mother's terrible rages. Pamela, when aroused, would dig her nails right into her hand so that it bled. This Louisa let out, when reproving me for my own anger over some trivial thing. She'd lie on the carpet and hammer at the walls, so May had heard said, happy to show up the family into which her young charge, my mother, had so recklessly married.

But Pamela is not on my mind when I come into the drawing-room from the garden steps. I have to get through the room, find my father, who will reach out his arms in a great welcome, and establish some equilibrium, some space for myself, in this room packed with the strange yet known monsters who are my family.

First, the smell must be conquered: the vases of lilies and phlox and roses that are overlaid by Clare's du Mauriers and the strong, sweet smell of gin from the drinks tray at the end of the drawing-room, where the fake bookcase with its whimsical titles stands in the wall. Then the particular smell of dry Martinis and flesh – the heat in the room, slow and reluctant at first from logs that Doug brings in, in a huge basket, grows rapidly as the drinkers glow, sweat, exude the pre-lunch drink that is now all the rage. (I have been taught to mix a dry Martini by my father: by the time he is on his second or third my mother's father, known as 'The Colonel' by Colin, is shouting the proportions, much as Clare master-minds the salad dressing, later, at lunch. 'One-eighth vermouth; seven-eighths gin.' And then, always up to date with the latest American craze, owner of a Thunderbird car in the stables here at Glen, my brother's correction: 'Just a breath of vermouth.' The Colonel, roaring in false appreciation, 'Oh, just breathe on it – oh, I say, that's perfect, that's good . . .'

Today, after receiving Clare's mysterious and wounding comment on my appearance, I make straight for the tray and lift a frosted, quickly warming shaker, add the last of the ice and pour in Gordon's gin. I know from experience – and especially from the visits of the writer L. P. Hartley (my mother invites writers to Glen, this in itself an invitation to further unpleasant comment from Clare) – that anyone who has had two Martinis already will easily drink four. It takes only a minute to swirl the contents around in the shaker. I cut another sliver of lemon peel at the request of one of the cousins and march round the room, armed – and protected – by the most desirable object in the room. My mother shakes her head; she looks sad at the braying of James, the shouting of The Colonel, and the brisk, self-satisfied crossword-solving of my brother, who sits in an admiring pose at Clare's feet. My father is also careful, and refuses another drink: it would certainly be quite out of character if this family man, Olympian and devoted, were to fail with the impossibly thin carving knife after the sounding of the gong for lunch. Otherwise, the contents of my shaker are happily accepted.

I lean right over Clare in order to reach her glass, and am sickened by the purple lipstick smudge on the tip of her cigarette. How can her son Harold (whose trunks, as supine as he is, never leave the attics at Glen: he is the TENNYSON who once baffled me, but now, with his brother Mark, a part of the regular August at Glen) – how can the 'boys', as my father calls these grown brothers (the younger, like his mother, in a family tartan kilt) stand her aloofness, her cigarettes, her hairnet and white, creamed face? But I can see from their anxious, loving expressions that they can; and I have to fight the feeling that I am the one who is 'wrong' here: I don't belong; as in the nursery rhyme read me by May when I was very young – of the old woman who goes to market, falls asleep under a tree on the way home and wakes to find her petticoats cut off up to the knee, then cries out, 'This is none of I!' – I am an alien here when the family comes, and have only Paula, a true outsider, to rely on.

But today Paula is roped in by Clare, to the world of gin, grown-ups and the promise of a game of canasta with the handsome, sociable Colin. Paula is laughing, telling Clare she has been talking of Harry Cust – the name electrifies me as it comes out and I glance guiltily at my father, though he gives no sign of having heard, sitting in benign judgment on his family. Did he know his mother had been in love with this beautiful and perfect-nailed man? I feel the deep unease of a trespasser on the past, when the present is agonising enough already.

'So brave of her to go up to Cust in Venice and say she knew he was her father,' says Paula.

'Who? Diana? Diana Cooper? Of course, she'd known for years . . .'

Clare snorts and grinds out her cigarette. I think of the daughter I've heard she never sees. I flinch, from the heat in the room and the underlying coldness she gives off. The gong in the hall gives a mighty boom.

* * *

131

So, as the austerity of the war years was succeeded by greater optimism and prosperity, Glen partly returned to its pre-war status: shooting in August; a place for the family to come to, fake plaid and all. Louisa stood in for the myriad servants once at the call of my father and his first wife, Pamela. We helped ourselves from a hotplate in the dining-room and shivered before pale one-bar electric fires.

It went without saying that Glen had to remain in the family – even if, as I saw with ever-increasing dismay, each member of that family hated at least one other with all their heart. (Were all families like this? The school friends I made – I was now in London during the term, at St Paul's – seemed not to be afflicted as I was. They lacked a 'glorious past' (my half-brother James's bragging speciality) and had many fewer divorces (Clare's Tennyson absolutely not mentioned, succeeded by an upper-class American, James Beck, who gave way in turn to an admirer known, muddlingly, as The General). Drink, in the shape of my Uncle David, whose one visit had him crawling to the brandy tray, at the shock, doubtless, of being away from London and the Gargoyle, didn't appear to figure high on the list of my friends' families' sins. Stephen was unlikely to remind anyone of *their* uncle.

I was alone; when I was with them I was 'none of I'. Yet when I was with my friends, I knew they thought me different from them – and all this, in an otherwise quiet and happy life at home, was as nothing, until the day, not more than a couple of years on from my first walk with Paula in the hills, when my elder half-brother Colin, already proving himself a worthy successor to the 'jewels' Pamela had brought into the world, announced to my horrified parents that he had invited Princess Margaret to Glen. She'd bring her maid Ruby, and a detective. She'd come in August, naturally.

EIGHT

The Daughter of an Emperor

Princess Margaret at Traquair Kirk, 1952

My younger brother Toby is in the process of being taught how to announce a telephone call to a royal personage. Eleven years old, already in full possession of every piece of knowledge Glen requires, in order to yield its secrets – where the deer roam, how the snipe and woodcock fly, in which pool lie the largest trout – he finds it hard to learn that, on being apprised by Louisa (or by the hired butler from Edinburgh) that a call has come through in the basement for the Princess, he must rise to the drawing-room and go in, bowing before divulging the news.

'On no account say, "Your mother is on the phone," ' hisses Colin – as apprehensive as the rest of us as to the outcome of this visit. 'Say, "Excuse me, Ma'am, Her Majesty Queen Elizabeth is on the telephone." ' Red-faced, stained by the winds and rain in which he spends his days, my younger brother nods but looks as if he can't really take the instructions in. With his usual tut of impatience, Colin sweeps down the hall, pausing more often nowadays under the big Constable of *Whitehall Stairs*, lingering by the Gainsboroughs, Romneys and portraits by Joshua Reynolds which will one day be his, entailed by Eddy through my father to his eldest son. Are the pictures, Sir Charles's prized collection, good enough for the 'Princiss'? – this, with a sibilant emphasis on the last syllable, is how my elder half-brother pronounces the name of the one who has catapulted our family into an unwelcome blaze of publicity. Will she – and here we none of us dare bring up the subject, though I feel it weighs heavily on my father and mother both – will Princess Margaret find my elder half-brother, after an introduction to his family and his pictures, a suitable man to marry?

The newspapers, laid out on the sideboard in the dining-room by Louisa, are more eager to speculate noisily than we are. The Scottish *Daily Express*, a paper given over almost entirely to snobbery and gossip, goes to town on our family: can they have a shooting photograph? Colin obliges: like real gentry, we stand in butts and lie back on family tartan rugs on sheep-nibbled grass while a nervous young man from Peebles presses the shutter of a camera so old-fashioned in appearance it could have been the one to record Eddy, Pamela and the 'jewels' when young. Could Colin give an interview? Certainly. My father sits in the library, drumming his fingers on the leather top of his desk. He has no comment to make to anyone. Only later, from the heights on which it is implicitly understood he has the right to dwell, will he suddenly – and perhaps conclusively – pronounce on the subject of his son's romance.

While all this is going on – detectives exploring the bushes; the Chief Constable, Mr Merrilees, coming to the house frequently, doling out free tickets for the Tattoo, an Edinburgh Festival speciality, performed in freezing rain at night below the castle and distinctly not a temptation; rooms dusted and scoured by Louisa with the help of three other women from Innerleithen – as the house designed as a showplace by the old Bart is prepared for its final glory, I wander off to the Walnut Room, and higher still to the boxrooms in pursuit of my search for the history of the century and of the family. Pamela, in the summer of 1915, teases Bim about the Regimental Ball, turns against the hell-kittens only to be reassured by her loving son that he thinks of no-one but her. A Zeppelin raid – the first – makes a great blaze in London, after the Season has come to an end and the rich and powerful have gone to their country estates. But Pamela, as I see from diaries and letters, stays on in London, at Mulberry House. Does she expect a reunion there? Does Harry Cust walk along Smith Square and look in at a lighted room, at Pamela bent over her letters at a desk? I no longer, at fifteen, pull out the photograph of the dead Hester, but she is there in my mind, born in the spring of the following year, when the snow is still on the ground at Glen. Colin said it was thought that most of Pamela's children were by men other than her husband, Eddy: surely, when I consider the unhappiness of Pamela, and, without knowing this is what I'm really interested in, the history of the women of the family, the longed-for second daughter must belong to Harry Cust? However Colin spoke against our grandmother, I wanted some respite from misery for her. That, at any rate, was my adolescent view of Pamela and for a long time I refused to believe her self-satisfied, narcissistic, a spoiler of her children, as my brother made her out to be.

Mr Merrilees liked to entertain the family, in the tense days before the arrival of the Princess. He stood in the drawing-room (my father, I think, was never

present on these occasions) and the Chief Constable
of Lothian and the Borders sang his ditties and delivered his jokes. 'You canny shove your granny off the
bus,' Merrilees sang loudly, as Toby looked away
bored and my mother and I giggled, showing in our
glances at each other that the world had gone mad:
how can it be, when life is normally so slow and
uneventful at Glen, that we are suddenly the captive
audience of a chief of Scotland's constabulary? But,
as we were discovering at a greater speed than we
liked, things had changed beyond all recognition
since my elder brother, described in the press as 'a
thing of beauty and a joy for ever', became (another
tabloid term) 'a close friend' of Princess Margaret.
My mother felt, I could see, 'this is none of I' at the
publicity; my father, wearing his most enigmatic and
hidden expression, saw perhaps the trail of sorrow
following Stephen's desperate search for 'grand success' – for interest provoked by the merely superficial,
the tawdry, the second-rate. He had no wish for my
elder brother, now basking in tabloid praise and sur-
rounded by an admiring crowd at all times, to suffer
the scorn and ridicule that later follow.

I am up in The Kennels looking down at the circular sweep of the drive when the royal car arrives. The
room, with its odd choice of scarlet valances and
chair-covers, its mural of animal heads dusted for the
coming of, in my brother's words, 'the daughter of an
emperor', and the general air of a room in which an
effort has been made, but to little avail, seems still to
contain the spirit of Pamela's communion with the
dead, her seances in which she found Bim again and
felt the brief brush of his hand on her shoulder, or his

lips against hers. There's an unnatural quietness here, for all that the car has stopped directly beneath us and the hired butler is visible as he runs down the steps to open the door. The rowan trees on either side of the front door, tall and covered now with August berries, sway in the wind but make no sound. The bald top of my father's head (he has to greet his son's important guest: his shoulders are stooped, still in his old green jacket, there's a limit to the changes he will make, however much our lives have been transformed) shows white as he also descends the steps, like a moon sinking against the shiny black of the royal car. His words of greeting are inaudible. Then my elder brother, dressed to the nines, darts down behind him and all three stand for what seems an age between the gargoyle-laden front porch and the pompous-looking conveyance. Despite the open window of this room, which has been allotted to an impecunious but, in Colin's terms, 'amusing' young heir to a barony, not a word, or a shuffle of shoe on gravel, can be heard.

The Kennels' door opens and Louisa comes in. She doesn't see me at first – I realise she must come up here often, to watch guests arrive, until it strikes me there is another reason for her familiarity with the room. She is mentioned in *The Earthen Vessel*, the book of my grandmother's. These are references in contemporary memoirs to the 'Scotch maid' who is brought south by the mother of Bim to assist in seances at Wilsford and London. Here, at Glen, must be where Pamela first detected Louisa's powers and made her one of the group of clairvoyants employed to bring back the dead. Louisa has more right than I to this room, with its unnerving silence and farcical décor: she 'owns' its past as I never could; and I see, as she makes her way almost absent-mindedly to the table in the centre of the room and gives it a flick with her duster as if this had been the true purpose of her visit, that she is thinking of someone. I've never seen her like this before – her whole face and being are drawn in, more than ever, against the present with its brutally hard work and its veneer of a past that can no longer exist. Louisa, as I suddenly understand, had been, and still is, in love with Bim.

We pass each other as if there is nothing out of the ordinary in this meeting high in the room where Pamela conjured the spirit of her son. I run down the back stairs; Louisa, still pretending to dust and tidy for the Honourable John Norton, remains behind. It's as I reach the main hall, breaking out from the obscurity and harshness of the back stairs into the green brightness of a large space filled with lilies and fuchsias in great pots – these brought in by old McNeil, retired now but desperate to please his wife, who wishes for no more than a glimpse of 'Margaret Rose' – it is as I blunder into the hall, thus forcing my brother to effect an introduction to the Princess, that for the first time I see my family from the outside. Clare, in tartan and cream silk shirt with string of pearls, is wobbling down into a curtsy as I come on the scene. 'The Colonel', puffing, his face the hue of a tropical sunset, stands ludicrously to attention by the door. My half-brother James, useless words pouring from his lips, is excelling himself today – and would no doubt already have received glares and frowns, were it not for the presence of the sister of the

Queen. The Tennyson 'boys', one plain, the other handsome, stand behind their mother like middle-aged pages at a wedding.

I may have experienced the sensation before, the 'none of I' feeling – but now, to my alarm and huge excitement, I experience my own transportation and translation to another realm altogether. I am split in two – more than I have been at the village school, where I must speak almost another tongue from that of my parents at the 'Big House'; more than the time when, confronted by the relic of my father's first loveless marriage, I was claimed by Pamela's Pamela for her own in the front hall. I can see the whole scene as if I am someone else entirely – and, as Louisa's head rounds the door from the back stairs (she is paler than ever but quietly satisfied, as if she has indeed met her ghost in the upstairs room), I understand that I can see the scene as Louisa sees it, as well as in my own way. I am torn in two – but now, at last, I can enter the past; I can imagine and depict it; I am a member of this family and yet I am no such thing.

Louisa circles the dining-table, set for this occasion with the gold candlestick (taken from the strong-room in the basement) and with the family silver, each spoon, fork and knife engraved with the ship in full sail, selected by Eddy when given his peerage by his brother-in-law H. H. Asquith in 1911; underneath are the words *Deus Dabit Vela* – a plea for a full sail but translated, an old family 'joke', as 'God give us wind', this invariably succeeded by groans and my half-brother James's interminable laughter.

Tonight no-one is laughing, least of all Louisa, as the unaccustomed circuit is made and the sauce-boats, impossibly ornate and scrolled, are handed with their precious accompaniments to the grouse: bread sauce, crumbs and strong, gamy gravy. She frowns, pausing by Clare who cannot resist smoking right through the meal, as Margot had; and she trembles a moment, glancing to the foot of the table as if she expects to see my grandmother there, a white goddess in simple lawn, emeralds that look as if they've been dragged out of the sea, a determined jaw setting off the dreamy beauty to which she aspires. And Eddy – Louisa sees him, the crinkle in his hair, the polite, almost too well-brought-up look about him, which leads men and women alike to pronounce with verve: 'Oh, Eddy had the most charm! And a mistress – in that house up the road – she was in love for years with Eddy . . .'

But Louisa sees my father, smiling at Princess Margaret, keeping his opinion of the whole affair to himself. He glances up at Louisa, keeps his same smile and waves on the indigestible condiments. She glides round, the tiny mustard, pepper and salt containers in their blue enamel and silver coats winking up at her, subjects of an intensive afternoon's polishing. Louisa is an old woman now. She knows, as I see, all the secrets of a past I can never understand or fathom except through her: it is she who must act as conduit for my desire to grasp history, just as she had steered the voice of Bim towards Pamela. She, of all people here, must hold the key to the decline of the family, the despair and frivolity that appear to affect each one but my father (and with him, too, she has seen the arranged marriage, the look of defeat of one of Pamela's children at obeying and loving his mother to the end). Louisa may know – but I can only guess. Meanwhile, my elder brother appears on the verge of changing the family fortunes beyond recognition by proposing to a member of the Royal Family. Whatever the outcome of this visit, I can feel my father's anxiety; see my mother's apprehension at the coming disruption of an otherwise quiet and unpretentious existence; most of all I sense Louisa's dismay – she who sees Colin where Bim once sat and cannot help but compare the seriousness, the love of poetry and willingness to sacrifice his life of my father's elder brother with the young man who sits there now.

The next days and their aftermath – some of this inexplicable to me: I roamed up to the loch while the family's future hung in the balance; my younger brother, Toby, out at all hours with gun and rod, an excellent antidote to the jokes, the canasta and the Martinis in the house at Glen – are best told back to me by Paula, who came to stay the following year when the débâcle of my elder brother's romance was long over and only the occasional *Daily Express* reporter emerged from a bush or drove right up to the loch, swearing at the way the road ends abruptly, newsless, by the foot of a hill. 'Darling, everyone says Colin *was* going to propose, you know. But your dear father – dear Christopher – asked him into the library. He said it was never too late to back out of a telling you – with such a fascinating woman. She was a poetess, married to the actor John Barrymore – she went by the name of Michael Strange.'

'I see,' I say. I don't really, of course: the past, with its dead rumours and incontrovertible facts, is poking out at me again and today I want to concentrate on what is still almost the present. My brother had gone to Balmoral from Glen, where the tabloids eagerly expected a proposal followed by the announcement of a Royal engagement.

'Colin in turn rushed to Venice,' Paula says, laughing. 'How naughty of the press, darling, to go to the casino and put him on the front pages of all those magazines – oh, I do so hope your brother won't end up simply gambling everything away!'

I am in a black car, as big and shiny as the car that brought my elder brother's 'Prin*ciss*' to Glen a few years before – but with something of the feeling of a hearse about it too, as it bears me and my companion, an elderly smiling lady, away from the present and into a past that predates the Second World War in which I have grown up.

We are in the Mall, stuck there in a queue of identical cars, all hired for the occasion. I am about, along with the other chubby faces in their limousines, to be presented at Court; and it comes to me, as we sit in a traffic jam and are peered in at by passers-by, that we might as well be stuck in the years before the First World War as the Second. For, as it happens, my mother is not permitted to be the one to show that I am now 'out'. Married to a divorced man and thus *persona non grata* in royal circles, she can only wave me goodbye as we set off for the Palace. I sense she is relieved at not having to face the Alice-Through-the-Looking-Glass duchesses, the stares of horse-faced women who felt they should have married Pamela's most eligible 'jewel' when he became free; and that she is as far from this world as I feel myself to be. Yet none of us queries the need for the pantomime: the hall table overflows with white pasteboard invitations engraved with the names of people of whom I have never heard. A ball near Malmesbury; a dance at the Hyde Park Hotel; a marquee in rainy June, a cold tent on uneven ground, a long drive home. I, without a murmur of dissent, will attend all these functions once my stint with the Queen has gone by. The press, still happy to needle us because of my half-brother's friendship with Princess Margaret, hints at proposals and engagements, compares me unfavourably with the 'Deb of the Year'. I know my parents are not entering me in the 'marriage market' on which the press likes to dwell pruriently. So why am I doing it? There seems to be no answer to this.

Along with a new interest in what is happening in the world around me has come an almost total loss of interest in the family's past. The days of excited rummaging, of dead babies and invented trysts, are utterly forgotten – if anything, the thought of my grandparents or great-aunt provokes distaste and an ever-growing desire to disassociate myself from all of them. Somehow, the accepted view of Pamela (not promulgated by my mother and father, who remain

silent on the subject) is that she is the villain of the
piece. Everything bad that befalls the family can be
traced back to her. A cross between the Whore of
Babylon and the Madonna, my grandmother was
fated to suffer the scorn of posterity. But, as with my
passive stance over the 'Season' on which I am about
to embark, I do nothing more than push the subject
from my mind. My grandmother, and my much-
vilified, much-married aunt Clare, have become
targets for the resentment and ridicule of younger
generations. It does not occur to me to think of them
in a more sympathetic light.

As it happens, this journey into the ancient rites of
protocol brings my feeling for the past suddenly back
to me. My 'presenter' at Court, Violet Wyndham –
daughter of Oscar Wilde's Sphinx, a writer, witty and
as far from the thick-headed minor nobility crushed
round us in the Mall as it is possible to be – is widow
of Pamela's brother Guy. (She has clearly been
chosen by my excommunicated parents because of
this, and for the above-mentioned qualities: perhaps
they foresaw my mounting dread in the black car
leading to the gates of Buckingham Palace.) As the
car inches forward, she smiles full into my face and
begins to tell me – I am too nervous, too foolish in my
green outfit to listen, at first – how much she loved
my grandmother. 'She was so kind – not only to me
but to everyone she cared for, you see. Pamela had
great charm – she was fascinating – but that wasn't
all. She had a good heart, she had no malice in her at
all.'

Now Violet begins to talk of Clare, and of her poor
daughter, abandoned by her mother since she was a

small child. 'In those days, you know,' says Violet in the mildest of tones, 'a woman's child would be taken from her at divorce – and this is what happened to your aunt. She wasn't allowed to see her little girl again – until she was eighteen, I think it was. By then it was too late, of course . . .'

The present lies, on this sunny day in late spring, like a golden haze about the cars and rigidly planted patriotic flower beds of the Mall. The day, unlike any day that has preceded it or will come after, is – as a child runs across the road and waves his arms, laughing at our sad-faced driver – only today, however much the Palace and its gold-tipped gates stand for the past. But, as Violet speaks, I glimpse my long-lost obsession: Pamela, walking from Queen Anne's Gate and a seance to raise her loved son; Sir Edward Grey, coming down Birdcage Walk from the Foreign Office; and Margot, tossing restlessly on her bed in Downing Street as a mob delirious for war, for change, for some kind of interruption to the brutal monotony of life, sings 'God Save the King' in snatches all through the night.

They are here. I sense the excitement of the gliding, jamming minute from another age before time straightens itself and goes on. We drive into the court-yard of Buckingham Palace, disembark and go into an assembly line of curtsying, canapé-nibbling girls. The moment has gone: for all their imposition of the past, the Royal Family on the dais look weary: this will be one of the last presentations at Court. I stand shamefacedly in line; Violet sits with the mothers on a gilt chair at the back. And I think I'm glad Pamela is exonerated: I'm happy she was kind.

NINE

A Visit
to my Uncle

Stephen Tennant, 1971

As the years pass, Louisa grows bent, hair as silver-brown as the underwings of the moths flushed from curtains and carpets by my sister-in-law, the new chatelaine, eyes shrunk in a web of fine lines over cheekbones now prominent in a wasted face.

Louisa has moved to the basement at Glen. Her aged father, even her odd niece Bella, are long dead. She prepares for the visits of my elder brother Colin and his wife and their two young sons. The wife, a Nordic beauty, an Earl's daughter whose lineage satisfies Colin, sits calmly at a desk in the drawing-room and writes letters. Her beauty reigns in a house now denuded of the actresses and long-dead great ladies of Sir Charles's collection – for Paula had been right in her apprehension that soon there would be nothing left of value at Glen. The famous pictures have gone, and many of the books from the library where my father sat drumming his fingers on the desk. Only the family portraits, rescued from attics and boxrooms whose contents have otherwise been auctioned off, remain in the house. Pamela and Eddy are in the Old Drawing-Room, restored to a sad marriage as they confront each other on walls no-one bothers to repaint. Sir Charles is still there – and now his daughters Charlotte and Margot flank him, bright-eyed with abundant tresses no-one would be seen dead in these days. A past has come to Glen – but at the price of the loss of all the secrets stored there. Rich plasterwork is uncovered on ceilings and cornices: where my father had boarded up, the grapes and lilies of a Victorian architect now stand revealed. Along with the moth-eaten and threadbare furnishings of the war years at Glen, unwanted pieces are thrown out. Reproduction William Morris replaces the tattered and faded draperies Louisa had washed and ironed from the days of the Great War up to the time of Lord Haw-Haw's broadcasts for Hitler, listened to by May and me with bewilderment. A new, fake past has come to settle on Glen, the place my elder brother has now had made over to him by our father and has never liked.

My visits only serve to make me think more of Pamela – and of Clare – and of Margot – and the lives they led here, in this castle, whose unreality and pretensions are now far more fully exposed by the new décor than they had been by my father's discreet hiding away of the past.

I wondered, as the tendencies of Pamela's 'jewels' (Stephen's dottiness; Clare's worldly desire for recognition and success; David's over-the-top nature with its rages and vast extravagances) became more marked with age, what could lie in store for a family where hatred and rivalry reappeared in the next generation with the virulence of the last. Strains in the children began to appear: my brother's elder son tormented by spirits, possessed by demons from an early age, able only to assuage his horror with drugs; his younger sibling as charming and frivolous as any in the family – and ultimately discovering himself to be gay, only to fall victim to AIDS. What worse fate could lie in store? And Pamela, as I'd heard, had somehow foreseen all this and had confided, as I was told, to an old friend that there would be trouble and she would be there, contactable, to give advice.

No-one seems to want this, in the Glen since her day. There are no seances in The Kennels; Louisa sends a young girl in to dust there, and the girl comes down the back stairs laughing, saying that the heads of dogs – and the great tusks of the boar – give her the spooks, when she's all alone at the top of Glen House. The spirit of Pamela has gone – and only Louisa is there to revive it.

I also forget. Only occasionally, when the 'jewels' reappear in my life, do I remember my longing, as a child, to crawl into the past, and my forays, over Harold's trunks and into the cupboard in the Walnut Room, to find my grandmother's world. I live in London and seldom go to Glen: I hear of my elder brother's disinheriting of his eldest son and appointment of the second son as heir – but I am inclined to think that it's hard to know what there is exactly for the boy to inherit. Glen, robbed of its secrets, cannot hold any value for me. Even the land, or a great deal of it, has been sold off by my half-brother from his palace on Mustique, the island he has invented that is as far from my father (by then living happily in Greece) as it is possible to go.

Perhaps it's thinking of my uncle and the occasion of the ball given for me by my parents all those years before that makes me decide to go down to Wilsford one summer day. Stephen had brought me a muff of gardenias for the dance that my parents gave for me when I was seventeen – my mother reminds me of this as we sit talking of that time one day, and she smiles as she says that the occasion had been so exciting to

Stephen that he ordered himself a gold lamé suit – *after* the ball, she says, and we both laugh. But I wonder if, living as a recluse, he has had an opportunity to wear it.

In June 1965 I decide to go down to the house on the Avon, the house loved above all else by my grandmother, and see.

Pamela, my grandmother, is in her garden. The photograph shows a woman in the cloche hat and low, belted dress of the early 1920s; the face is smooth, and the jaw more pronounced than in the dreamy pictures of years before the war. The sun is shining: whoever holds the camera is a favourite, neither a stranger nor a threat.

Behind Pamela lies the mock village green she created when Wilsford was built for her by Eddy. Like an aura, a halo, the sunlight encircles the whiteness of Pamela's face. Her death, in this garden, is less than half a decade away. But Bim's terrible death – along with so many others in the September battle of the Somme – is written as clearly by the white sun on her face as if it had been worked there by a knife in marble.

It is winter, and a protective wall behind Pamela hosts espaliered trees, apricot and peach. No shadows are visible anywhere: the dark runnels of shade cast by the fake dovecote at the side of the green are out of the frame: the racquet court, disguised as cottages for the rural population Pamela loves to mimic, to cover with kindness, to ignore, has birds strutting on the picturesquely tiled roof. Another, deeper shadow, from the Norman church of Wilsford – real this time, but just as easily seen as a part of the fantasy of those years – lies just beyond the glare of wall and light where Pamela sits. A young coachman, Louis Ford, emerges from the stables and comes into the walled garden, to ask if the carriage is needed. He must go for provisions to Salisbury. And Pamela, knowing the reason for the sudden, unpredictable shortage of supplies at the manor – and recalling the ecstasy of the servants and the children as they ran away from Wilsford at dawn and up on to the downs, to arrive at Stonehenge at the rising of the midsummer sun and return famished, to eat the larder bare – smiles now at Louis and tells him to take the carriage. She knows he will never learn to drive a car, though David's Alvis sits in the stables and Salisbury can now be reached in fifteen minutes. Louis, for all his youth, belongs to the past.

It is Louis I first see when I arrive at Wilsford. It's a strange arrival: told that a cottage lies empty by the River Avon, I've come down from London in a small furniture van. My companion is the playwright Heathcote Williams; he's just completed the play that ignites the '60s – *AC/DC* – and he's brought as luggage a large radio and no more. He's promised to help unload two beds, a table and some rudimentary cooking utensils, so that I can move into this possible cottage – my friend Mark will come later.

The cottage – constructed by my father from two abandoned rural slum dwellings and definitely not a part of Pamela's William Barnes rustic dream – seems at first not to exist. All I know of it, as we drive down the narrow road, where ivied trees allow light in blinding flashes or not at all, is that it was put together as a new home for Stephen, to cut costs. Wilsford had long been far too expensive for this eccentric solitary to run, if 'run' was a word that could ever apply to my uncle. Here, only a few hundred yards from the old house he had always lived in, was the solution. Teasels had been Pamela's most loved wild flower. My father, in a revealing burst of sentimentality, had apparently named this uninhabited building 'Teasel Cottage'.

The building was uninhabited because Stephen had refused to move into it. Worse, it was said he had not even bothered to walk along the riverbank and see what his elder brother had put together for him. And now, to make matters worse still, the place had apparently disappeared altogether.

Louis came out of the back door into the stable yard at Wilsford and stared in apprehension at the van and the wild physiognomy of Heathcote Williams. The van driver wanted a pee. The deep stillness of Wilsford – even here at the rear there was the sense of thicket and briar, of a hundred years' sleep rudely punctured – resumed as we backed out and drove on down the thin, green ribbon of tarmac that runs between the two houses built by Eddy and Pamela, Wilsford and Lake – and on down the Woodford Valley to Salisbury. I knew I would have to introduce myself later to Louis – and the picture of his face, puckered in great age, crowned by white hair, remained uncomfortably with me. People came quite often, I told myself – people who had less right than I to disturb the peace of the mock village green, almost derelict now, as I had glimpsed, a village-that-never-was reduced to a ruin no-one could ever want to repair. People came, demanding to see my uncle Stephen. But it was well known that he would see no-one at all.

The van driver brakes suddenly. There is a modern wooden garage in a small bay by the side of the road, on a dangerous bend. No sign, no indication of what may lie beyond it – but we know by now that it's the only construction between Wilsford and Lake. And as we pile out, to stand under trees of an alarming height, I see the roof of the cottage my father went to so much unrewarded trouble to make. Thatch lies under the bank like the back of a well-groomed animal. There is even a kind of hair-net on it. A virtually invisible path winds down beyond the garage: we follow it, in a gloom of trees untended since the days of Eddy's stewardship of the place forty years ago.

Our emergence on the terrace in front of the cottage makes us blink, then gasp and shout. What would have been Stephen's view – water meadows, gentle hills in the distance, the silver loop of the Avon as it winds down to the weir at Lake – will now (but how, for how long? Like everything connected with my uncle, these questions are unanswerable) be mine.

We open the door and go in. A long room, with beams that have been stripped; a bright wooden floor; and doors at each end so wide that a procession could have walked through them. (Wide doors were a fad of my father's – and indeed his influence is everywhere, in this new construction from old materials.) The symmetry of two staircases, one at each end of the cottage, each leading to two bedrooms and a bathroom, the evenly spaced windows and the well-planned kitchen all spoke of an architect's eye, coupled with the neatness and balanced view of the world that belonged to the only one of the brood who had gone at twelve years old to Dartmouth College, and thus away from Pamela.

Teasel Cottage was a triumph of good financial sense and economy of space. The fact that it was empty only underlined the folly of self-indulgence into which my uncle had descended. But, stooping slightly to look from the deep-set windows on to the terrace and beyond it to the river, at the foot of a sloping expanse of grass, was to begin to understand why 'normal behaviour' would be difficult, if not impossible, to achieve here – and Stephen had not gone through life under the label of 'normal' in any case. It was too operatic here: even the path that wound along the side of the Avon was of a jewelled, unnatural green. The tangle of giant yellow flag iris, bamboo and rushes that made up the land lying between Wilsford and the cottage grounds looked like an unconvincing stage set. Anyone who had spent their life in these surroundings – and especially Stephen, with his adoring mother Pamela – would continue to expect a pageant, a pantomime, every time he went out of the house. The knowledge that the old stones lay up above the manor – that a walk over the downs led directly to Stonehenge, with all its terrifying associations – would add unbearably to the sense of melodrama in the place. I began to see more clearly: my uncle was as pinioned, in the old house guarded by Louis Ford and by his piles of past clothing, cuttings and memorabilia, as a Bronze Age victim of a Druidic rite on his slab of stone. There was no getting away from it: Stephen was made for Wilsford, just as he had taken it over at his mother's death and fashioned it for no-one but himself.

It was very hot – midsummer – and we all ran down to the water, Heathcote Williams stripping off energetically as we went. The van driver, with Heathcote's help, had carried in the few bits of furniture and was certainly the hottest of us three – but even he, as we came to the river bank, hesitated before announcing that he was going off instead in search of a pub. Someone had said there was one beyond Lake, at Great Durnford. He waved, turned on his heel, and was gone.

For a moment I stand alone on the path, staring up at the cottage and taking in for the first time the small red-brick house perched above it on the perilous road. My father had mentioned an 'old schoolhouse' – I wonder whether Pamela's children, spending so much of the year in their mother's beloved Wilsford, took lessons there. Perhaps Clare, always eager to move on, away from Pamela – to new men, new sensations, new ways of squandering and regretting – had sat there, her beautiful face pale with boredom on the long summer afternoons. I try to remember if I was told about a governess – but then, as Clare vanishes from my sights, I glimpse something that moves, in the grey-green wash of willow that borders the river path. It moves – then is gone – then flashes bright again, greener than any emerald, eyes blue as the crude backdrop of the sky.

'Oh yes, a tree frog,' says Heathcote, who is now wading – and grinning in enjoyment at the mud that rises in black circles about his knees. 'Very common round here, so I'm told.'

Of course the animal is not a tree frog and Heathcote's imagination is already providing him with a bestiary for this improbable tropic. It's a lizard – and I see several more, on the path itself this time – streaks of the enamelled green seen only on Chinese porcelain. I see, too, why the van driver preferred the dark comforts of the local pub: the lizards, though small, are unsettling, out of place, in what should be a typically English scene of chalk stream, water meadow, accommodating cattle and even a pair of swans. By now, though, the appearance of a reptile with sky-blue eyes seems more in keeping with the landscape than the rest.

'Escaped from my uncle's Snake House,' I invent – and yet I do now remember hearing Stephen beg my father, on a rare visit to London during the war, for 'something to go with my reptiliary – a seal pond – Christopher, wouldn't it be *fun?*'

If Heathcote is fazed by the thought of further escaped inmates from my uncle's neglected zoo, he doesn't show it. The swans glide by; he climbs from the mud; and, looking, if possible, wilder than before, he joins me on the journey to Wilsford by way of the river bank. A broken-down boathouse lies a few hundred yards ahead; just before it a wooden bridge, rickety and grown round by iris and swamp weed, leads up towards the garden and the chequered façade of the manor. Already, as we make our way cautiously across the cuts, on bridges that prance like stilt-walkers in the ooze of summer-dry streams, I feel the silence return: the sleep; the sense, in each faint rustle of bamboo clump or overgrown azalea, of a hidden, waiting presence.

The lawn at Wilsford – the lawn that forms a travelling-rug, tattered in places, pulled up almost to the shadows of the dining-room and drawing-room at the back, and spread sparsely down the shanks of land as far as the reed beds encroaching on the river – is run across by Heathcote, who laughs and grimaces as he goes, as if aware that a hand may come suddenly from the grey upper regions of the house and pull him in.

I follow at a slower pace. Perhaps the imp Heathcote has become, mud-faced from the Avon, hair in a mad mop, eyes aslant so that he resembles a green man of early German sculpture, a goblin, a creature made from the stuff of the surrounding trees and water, knows somehow that he will be greeted kindly by my uncle. Whereas I, for all my kinship with the resident of Wilsford Manor, will not be taken to at all. It is unheard of for a woman visitor to gain admittance, or so I have heard said. Jokes have been made about the occasion of a visit from two literary women, Rosamund Lehmann one of them, genuine recipients of an invitation from Stephen to visit Wilsford. They were greeted at the door with the astonished comment, 'How could you have taken me so cruelly literally?' It is foolish of me to approach in this way, even if I do bring messages from my father: that I am permitted to become his brother's neighbour; that my presence will not disturb Stephen in the least. I have a strong feeling that Stephen would never have noticed my occupancy of Teasel Cottage – that my father is quite wrong to imagine him as still interested in the dip of land beyond the trees where Pamela planted snowdrops and aconites to brighten winter days. Stephen cares for the flowers, he may stroll a little way under the beeches in February, but he would never come as far as the banned cottage. The short walk would take him from youth to the reality of old age.

I am apprehensive, trying to remember the visit I made here with my mother when I was a child of ten. A late spring, hot again; the nervous expression on my mother's face when, she and I sitting in the dining-room at a table covered in shells, she looked up at the window to see Stephen there, plump-cheeked, florid and lion-haired, a posy of bluebells pressed to each side of his face. She wanted me then, I think, to see the strangeness of the place – even, as a comfort, to laugh secretly with her – but I was too young to find the place or atmosphere unusual: I had paid few visits to other houses; and most grown-ups seemed strange to me. My uncle ran in then, after making the apparition at the window, and placed on my finger what looked like a raindrop on a leaf. The transparent drop didn't tremble or slide away. He said it was a moonstone – and spoke with deep emotion. My mother looked up at the ceiling, where more shells were embedded, each gilt-edged, softly pink and blue as if lapped by the seas of Stephen's distant travels. Mrs Ford came in, with chicken and bread sauce, the most English of meals. But there was nowhere to put the dishes, amongst the conches and cowries all around. These memories are not reassuring, and I find myself increasing my pace, running the last stretch across a lawn designed for an Edwardian tea-party. The cedar, supported by an iron crutch, has outlived the heroes of the Somme; a paved garden, complete with palm trees, seems ready for a band to play, a girl to step from the french windows in the inevitable muslin dress. But here, as on the river bank, everything seems to have changed, to be both exotic and unsurprising, like the jewelled lizards running free from my uncle's reptiliary. Sand the colour of a wartime postcard sunset is scattered in the tiled loggia beyond the drawing-room windows. What looks like hibiscus and bougainvillaea make a lurid splash against the walls of a sagging conservatory. A copper heron covered in green slime stands one-legged in a dripping pool. The country-house idyll has gone to Hollywood, and there has faded, rusted and run riot, so that Pamela's box-hedged walks and mellow kitchen garden are no more than traces of the past.

My father never spoke of his mother, yet I am at once aware – as we follow a gesticulating Louis through the great soft door that separates Stephen's Wilsford from that of cooking smells, walls of institutional green, a snug little parlour where Mrs Ford, lifting a hand to wave (they are still not sure who I am), sits ensconced with knitting and goldfish in a bowl – that the pictures on wall, piano and low tables everywhere are pictures of Pamela. The house is a shrine to her: she is a dark deity, serious stubborn face and few signs of the beauty and sex appeal to which so many admirers testify. Alone, or encircled by her children, slim-waisted, soberly dressed, Pamela looks out from every angle at the interior that once had been hers, white-walled, William Morris-plain, and now is a gaudy temple to the pleasures of the bright and ephemeral.

Louis is talking as he goes. His speech is fast, confused and hard to understand. But he's working it out for himself: asked if I am 'David's daughter', I see him reach my identity before I can find a space in his incessant flow to set him right. With hands clad in white cotton gloves (he also wears a white cotton jacket, as if preparing to serve cocktails on a cruise liner), he indicates the excesses of Stephen's arrangements in the downstairs rooms at Wilsford. It occurs to me that the Fords know themselves to be curators of a singular taste – as was the custom in the eighteenth century when a stranger, coming to the door of a great house, would be admitted and shown around with no questions asked – that it gives them pleasure to play host while Stephen lies immobile in his room. It comes back to me, almost guiltily – as family anecdotes, ignored at the time but found to be relevant later, are inclined to do – that my father had expressed exasperation with Stephen's habit of letting in any rogue 'antique dealer' to Wilsford. In exchange for a pocketful of cash, he had apparently

parted with Meissen birds, with a Chelsea dinner
service, and had even seen carried out of the door a
Sheraton sideboard and valuable chairs. Word of
Louis Ford's amicability when it came to paying a
call at Wilsford must have got around speedily.

What the 'connoisseurs' had left was, indeed,
pretty tatty. Polar-bear rugs, once glamorously lain
on by famous people, now bore the unmistakable
brownish patches of a pet dog – or perhaps another
escaped inmate of a long-abandoned cage. Sofas in
their white satin covers were similarly afflicted.
Venetian console tables, presumably fixed to the wall
and to the elegant ormolu mirror above them and
thus a harder proposition when it came to a jingle of
florins and a quick getaway, were chipped and misty.
If the garden from which we had just come showed
some ghosts of order, design and well-chosen plant-
ing, then the interior of Wilsford certainly did not.

Things have gone far beyond what they had been
when I last came here. Then, despite the pervading
presence of puce- and magenta-striped wallpapers,
cornices ablaze with what appeared to be gold cake-
braid, wide banisters of a fine pale wood obscured
with draped fish nets, like a Brighton restaurant,
there had been room to walk and sit, to examine
Stephen's 'treasures' as he had laid them out. Now,
with an Eastern sense of the equality of importance
between an object and a medley of paper flowers, all
distinctions have disappeared. Where there had been
shells, coral and the remnants of *objets de vertu* from
his father's and grandfather's collections, there is
now a jumble of ties, silks in bales that spilled from
Bangkok suitcases, old photos of Hedy Lamarr and

an assortment of journals, open to the scared eye of the viewer, each entry in a different-coloured Indian ink.

Louis pulls me along a passage that leads under an arch from the hall drawing-room, and we stand under the shells upon which my mother had gazed so earnestly on the occasion of Stephen's appearance at the window with the bluebells. He is talking – he is trying to tell me something while chuckling with glee – and I realise he is telling me of the morning, all those years ago, when he and the other servants and the children went up to Stonehenge at dawn to see the sun strike the sacrificial slab. The white-gloved hands point excitedly in the direction of the front sweep to Wilsford; the low gate that leads to the churchyard where Pamela lies in her Rex Whistler-designed grave; the way to the pale blue sky over the downs and the old drove road. There had been nothing left to eat, after they had wolfed down the contents of the larder on their return. The carriage – Louis spits the word, makes galloping movements with his arms in the white cotton jacket that is far too short – he needed to take it into Salisbury to make up the loss, but he'd left it too late and had to ask if he could go, instead of just slipping off there.

As I stand listening to the tale, I see, on a table piled with junk in the dining-room, the photograph of Pamela in her garden. I see her frown – and then smile at Louis when he admits the plunder that has taken place. He is tugging at my arm now – he wants to show me that same carriage in the stables. What can I do but oblige him and go?

My instinct to remain and keep an eye on

Heathcote, however, proves to have been right. I feel a desire to get out of this place, with all the uncomfortable questions it gives rise to. (For Pamela, as the presiding presence, is so powerful that I have to ask why my father does not speak of her: is it because his first wife, Pamela's god-daughter and also named Pamela, is now unmentionable? Does that marriage, engineered by his mother, between the daughter of one of her many suitors and the son who followed the sainted Bim as eldest son of the family, demonstrate only too conclusively the power Pamela exercised everywhere? Is my father still afraid of her? And, if so, what does this mean?)

The questions are, as always, unanswerable. But they press on me and I want to leave. The straightforward lines and total lack of mystery in the cottage just a stone's throw down the valley begin to seem more and more inviting. Besides, Louis is gesturing to the upper floors, is dragging me out to the hall again and beginning to mount the stairs. Surely – and I become increasingly panic-stricken at the thought – he cannot want me to go up, to risk a meeting with Stephen? The fact that I was not greeted downstairs has already confirmed my suspicion that he has no desire to see a niece, particularly one who might make a habit of coming over and disturbing his peace – or his beauty regime; my distracted eye catches an entry in gentian ink in a logbook in one of the arrangements near the foot of the stairs: 'Rest the eyelashes for a month. My resolution: no mascara, no eye pencil . . .'

Of course, it is too late. Louis, clearly accustomed to conducting any passing burglar to the upper quarters, has news of a more urgent nature to communicate. I run up now, fearing what I will find there.

Yet again, my sense that it is I my uncle dreads, turns out to be correct. In the bedroom – I stop on the landing, despite all Louis's tugs and pulls – I see the end of a great bed, a part of a room where more piles of bright mementoes are gathered, on the floor and on a vast sofa where not one inch remains for any person to sit, and I hear a rustling, as if tissue paper is in the process of being gently pulled apart. Another memory comes to me – a letter from Mrs Ford to my father: his rueful laugh; and, on my mother's demanding to know what the matter can be, the reply that 'the Fords have found a nest of twelve mice in Stephen's bed'. My mother's reaction: 'Oh *no* –' and my father exchanging glances with me, to see if I laugh, which I do.

Louis looks round the door like a child. He's enjoying himself: he puts his finger to his lips to enjoin silence.

The rustling sound turns out to be tissue paper after all – bright pink and mauve, like everything in this house. Everything here is devoted to murdering memory and keeping it intact at the same time.

I see Stephen – but then I look away quickly, for I think at first I see an old woman there. Fat, radiant with self-love, this apparition has long, unwashed hair. I see that Heathcote is perched on the end of my uncle's bed. He wears a sardonic expression, as Stephen, unwrapping the gift packaging, reveals his treasures: a cameo ring, a little blue enamel clock with gold hands; suddenly, a plain pigeon's feather.

Heathcote looks up and sees me. Stephen, intent on his trove, does not.

As we walk down the road to the wooden garage in its bay, I wonder if Stephen is even now feeling disappointed that a shower of coins did not meet his wares.

TEN

A Funeral

Christopher Tennant in 1919, aged twenty

No-one really seems to know when my father was born – 14th June, say some; on the white china mug with gold lettering, which he was careful to take with him to the house by the sea in Greece, 16th June is proclaimed as his date of birth. (Did Pamela not know or care?) But the death of Christopher, third child of Eddy and Pamela, took place on 4th October 1983 – in a clinic in Corfu town decorated with eighteenth-century caryatids, which look down a sloping street to the blue sea he loved to paint. After a journey by aeroplane, a cremation and the necessary wait of an interminable Scottish bank holiday, my father's ashes will finally be laid to rest in the kirkyard at Traquair, a mile up the road from Glen. The minister will speak of a 'golden age' (he wasn't in this neck of the woods himself). Colin will sit and stare straight ahead in the front pew, his recent facelift giving him an expression of surprise at this tactless assertion.

Louisa sits at the back, waved there by the solemn ushers who seem to have sprung from the ground like black trees. Mrs McKay is dead, but her daughter who lives not far away has come to join the small band of mourners; and one of the shepherds, from the far-distant cottage up the glen behind the loch, has brought his collie, which stands patiently just outside. Otherwise, there is little trace of the near-century of Glen that my father represents, in the little kirk where Margot loved to visit the grave of old Sir Charles and feel the pearly air of a Peeblesshire day turn to sudden gale or

magnificent, blue-vaulted sky. Bim, who is commemo-
rated in Salisbury Cathedral, has left no roots there:
Pamela placed his plaque in her own country, far from
the rudeness of Scotland or the tragic geometry of the
war dead in France. Pamela herself lies at Wilsford,
beneath snowdrops, bluebells, wild garlic and the
pretty shells and flowers engraved on her tomb. This
graveyard and kirk are for the family before Pamela.

Scottish funeral services are short and to the point
and we all file out, into an October day so garishly
beautiful it could be cut up into pieces and rearranged
as a jigsaw. Rowans and beeches are a fiery red, the
grassy slopes of the valley look ready to roll down, to
land in the purple shadows at their base, and the hills
where once Clare looked out in frustration at her
imprisonment at Glen lie like pipe-smoking men,
brown-suited, in their wait for the long white spell of
winter.

My father is last but one of Pamela's children to die.
Clare has been dead over twenty years, coming north
to Glen and to the Walnut Room in order to die in her
brother's arms (I would take her in a Martini every day
before lunch: Why not, said the doctor, shrugging
when asked what a heart patient should and should not
consume). Stephen will die in four years' time at
Wilsford, and will be said to haunt the place. His ghost
will need to be exorcised by a local bishop in order to
facilitate works carried out by the new owners. David,
brought over from his retreat in the south of Spain, is
buried at Wilsford, like his mother and like Sir Oliver
Lodge, the instigator of Psychic Research and many of
the seances Pamela expected her son to attend. On the
day of his funeral, a barn owl, Pamela's most loved and

protected bird, flapped down the old drove road from Stonehenge, past Springbottom Farm and right to the edge of the churchyard, so green and enclosed, so different from the kirk on its hillside here, before going off lazily, following the course of the Avon to the weir.

Pamela is everywhere, in the South – but here, as the ashes are interred and a dour-faced man in black looms suddenly above me as I walk past the grave, in need of the icy air which blows in over the hills from Siberia, there is no sense of her at all. My father's ashes lie now beneath a wreath of gentians from my mother, the alpine blue as strong and encouraging as the happy years of his life had been to him. Pamela, his mother – a mythological creature still to me, by reason of his decision never to speak of her – has finally by this, his last silence, been dispersed. Like his date of birth, she can cause an archaeological controversy, she can be labelled, described; and in the metamorphosis that will befall her each time a new generation attempts to discover and delineate her, she will change beyond recognition.

A family scene is taking place by the wicket gate that leads up to the graveyard, the white shape of the manse beyond. My elder half-brother's wife, dressed smartly in jet-black two-piece with fashionable hat (my mother, younger sister and I in our macs resembling bagwomen by comparison – or so her haughty demeanour suggests), is crying histrionically and seizing the sleeve of my younger brother, Toby, a farmer across the hills in the Borders, in an attempt to force a 'reconciliation' between him and my elder half-brother. Colin's sale of land attached to Glen has brought yet another feud to the family. She sobs; but her display of grief surprises rather than moves me. Both men, embarrassed, shake hands – I'm almost surprised there is no photographer there to record the occasion.

To remove myself from the scene, I circle the sloping burial ground, avoiding my other half-brother James, to whom no-one at all appears prepared to speak. I go high, to look across at the hills of Glen, the tombstones of Sir Charles's daughters and sons at my feet, and return to the grave where Mrs McKay's daughter and Louisa remain, pious and stiff, uncertain as to what to do next. And I see the wreath, concealed before by the rest of the flowers and now left, undying, on grass by the graveside that is freshly filled in.

The wreath, of British Legion red poppies, has a card from Pamela, my father's first wife, carefully tied on. 'In memory of the *Lord Nelson*' runs the message; and I stand a moment there in surprise, at this sudden reminder of the First World War, and of the ship in which my father served as a midshipman, at Gallipoli.

Pamela's Pamela, looking back across the century to those days, has chosen to mark her husband's death (to the end she called him 'my Christopher') with the red poppies of Remembrance Day.

I don't go to Glen for the wake, but am driven instead to Edinburgh, to the airport and thence to London. As I fly south, I think of the Walnut Room, and the attics with Harold's trunks, and the floral packet where Pamela kept all her most precious letters. I need to write, of my long-ago obsession with the past and with the family – and I begin to set down what I've remembered, and what I've been told. All I need is to find the words for what had taken so long to forget and now takes an age to remember.

Postscript

It's February 1986. I'm in my house in west London, preparing for a move. Books and dusty plates are piled on the floor and my daughters, running from floor to floor, pile their things into cardboard boxes.

An album spills out pictures – Colin at Glen in a Beatles wig (this can only be from the '60s, when he had just taken over the place); my sister Catherine, like a koala bear, being held and hugged in the garden where the stone plaque, PAMELA HER GARDEN, is set in the wall above the wooden bench that always tips down like a seesaw when someone sits there who isn't in the know. Myself and my elder half-brother's wife, on a low, white-washed wall just outside the drawing-room steps where Paula and I, fresh from my first 'grown-up' conversation, walked in to a room of gin and heady herbaceous scent.

There is one photograph of Glen, taken from the top of the garden, where the iron gate was taken off in the war. I wonder, as I push it back into the shabby folder, how I could possibly have spent my childhood, often almost on my own, in this fantastical Disney castle, forbidding, frivolous and cold.

The doorbell rings. Before I can rise from the floor, my nephew Henry is in the room, immensely tall, thin and feverish, an AIDS victim in need of advice and help.

What can I do for him? I suggest the name of a doctor and we sit facing each other. It's impossible not to think of his approaching fate, of the brave, capable and intelligent widow and son he will leave behind; and of Glen, made over to him some years since by my elder half-brother and now let out as a conference centre, only the basement and library kept for the family's use.

'There's something I feel impelled to tell you,' Henry says.

His eyes shine, he smiles in a way that alarms me: it occurs to me that he is affected already by the virus and doesn't know what he will say, or why.

'You see,' Henry says, 'I have to tell you. It's a secret – a secret I really want you to know.' He comes towards me, kneels on the floor – and, as he whispers, I am transported back to the Walnut Room cupboard: to the letters and diaries and photographs which made up the stories I concocted there, about Pamela and her children.

How much of what I thought then is truth, and how much fantasy? As with the dreams and documents that fed my obsession with the past, there is no way of saying that what is true to me is not also history.

Now, as Henry goes on with his own version of the family romance, I smile, hoping to reassure and calm.

Yet, as he leaves and I make my way through the emptied cupboards and stacked pictures of my imminent move, I cannot help but remember the day when I was three years old in the front hall at Glen, and the strange woman who said she was my mother held me captive there for a frozen minute. Who am I now? I think of the tale of the old woman on the way back from market, petticoats cut off to her knee, and I put my hand on Henry's arm as we walk out to the door. All I know is that it is none of I.

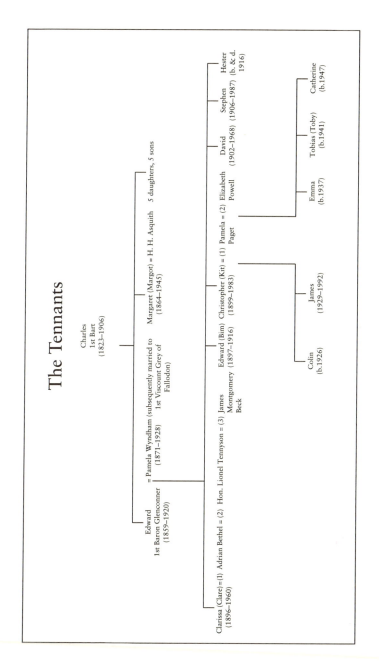

The Tennants

Charles
1st Bart
(1823–1906)

Edward = Pamela Wyndham (subsequently married to   Margaret (Margot) = H. H. Asquith   5 daughters, 5 sons
1st Baron Glenconner   (1871–1928)   1st Viscount Grey of   (1864–1945)
(1859–1920)   Fallodon)

Clarissa (Clare) =(1) Adrian Bethel = (2) Hon. Lionel Tennyson = (3) James   Edward (Bim)   Christopher (Kit) = (1) Pamela = (2) Elizabeth
(1896–1960)   Montgomery   (1897–1916)   (1899–1983)   Paget   Powell
Beck

Colin   James   Emma   David   Stephen   Hester
(b.1926)   (1929–1992)   (b.1937)   (1902–1968)   (1906–1987)   (b. & d.
1916)

Tobias (Toby)   Catherine
(b.1941)   (b.1947)

183